Translation and Norms

Edited by
Christina Schäffner

MULTILINGUAL MATTERS LTD
Clevedon • Philadelphia • Toronto • Sydney • Johannesburg

British Library Cataloguing in Publication Data

A CIP catalogue record for this book is available from the British Library.

ISBN 1-85359-438-5 (hbk)

Multilingual Matters Ltd

UK: Frankfurt Lodge, Clevedon Hall, Victoria Road, Clevedon BS21 7HH.
USA: 325 Chestnut Street, Philadelphia, PA 19106, USA.
Canada: 5201 Dufferin Street, North York, Ontario M3H 5T8, Canada.
Australia: P.O. Box 586, Artamon, NSW, Australia.
South Africa: PO Box 1080, Northcliffe 2115, Johannesburg, South Africa.

Printed and bound in Great Britain by Short Run Press Ltd.

Contents

Christina Schäffner: The Concept of Norms in Translation Studies   1

Gideon Toury: A Handful of Paragraphs on 'Translation' and 'Norms'   9

The First Debate   32

Theo Hermans: Translation and Normativity   50

The Second Debate   72

Andrew Chesterman: Description, Explanation, Prediction: A Response
to Gideon Toury and Theo Hermans   90

Daniel Gile: Norms in Research on Conference Interpreting: A Response
to Theo Hermans and Gideon Toury   98

Anthony Pym: Okay, So How Are Translation Norms Negotiated?
A Question for Gideon Toury and Theo Hermans   106

Douglas Robinson: Looking Through Translation: A Response to
Gideon Toury and Theo Hermans   113

Sergio Viaggio: The Limitations of the Strictly Socio-Historial
Description of Norms: A Response to Theo Hermans and
Gideon Toury   122

Gideon Toury: Some of Us Are Finally Talking to Each Other.
Would it Mark the Beginning of a True Dialogue? Comments
on Responses   129

Theo Hermans: Some Concluding Comments on the Debates and
the Responses   133

The Concept of Norms in Translation Studies

Christina Schäffner
Institute for the Study of Language and Society, Aston University, Birmingham B4 7ET

The Concept of Norms

In the long history of translation, such notions as accuracy, correctness, or well-formedness have played an important role in assessing the quality of a translation. Depending on what is understood by translation, these notions have been given different significance. Despite much research over the past 50 years, translation studies has not developed into a homogeneous discipline and there is no agreement on its central concepts. Different approaches exist side by side, each of which focuses on specific aspects, looks at the product or the process of translation from a specific angle, and uses or avoids specific terminology. One of the concepts that has been used differently within translation studies and whose value has been both asserted strongly and called into question, is the concept of norms. Both Gideon Toury and Theo Hermans have contributed substantially to this debate and to the development of the concept of norms in and for translation studies. They are the two main contributors to this *CILS* issue which is based on a seminar on 'Translation and Norms' held at Aston University in February 1998.

Research within translation studies has been concerned with the description of actual translations, with the formulation of general principles, and with practical applications. Norms play a role in all these respects since they are related to assumptions and expectations about correctness and/or appropriateness. Bartsch (1987: xii) defines norms as 'the social reality of correctness notions'. That is, in each community there is a knowledge of what counts as correct or appropriate behaviour, including communicative behaviour. In a society, this knowledge exists in the form of norms. Norms are developed in the process of socialisation. They are conventional, they are shared by members of a community, i.e. they function intersubjectively as models for behaviour, and they also regulate expectations concerning both the behaviour itself and the products of this behaviour.

Bartsch (1987), who applied the norms concept to linguistics, differentiates between product norms and production norms, which, however, are closely related. Product norms regulate what a product must look like in order to be regarded as correct and appropriate. They concern the correctness and the well-formedness of linguistic expressions (i.e. linguistic norms as related to the language system) as well as the correctness of their use (i.e. communicative norms as related to communicative behaviour). Production norms concern the methods and strategies by which a correct product can be achieved (cf. the 'operational norms' in Toury (1995: 58).

Language and language use can be judged as correct from a phonological, morphological, syntactic, semantic and pragmatic point of view. There is also a difference between what is possible in a language, regardless of context (described by rules), and what is considered appropriate in a given context

1

(described by conventions or norms). When conventions are enforced with normative power they are considered to be norms. Norms are binding, and their violation usually arouses disapproval of some kind among the community concerned. The force of a norm is built up in the relationships between norm authorities, norm enforcers, norm codifiers, and norm subjects. For example, grammar books and lexicons provide models for correct linguistic forms, language teachers correct wrong or inappropriate communicative behaviour, or teachers of translation judge a text to be a good or a bad translation.

In translation studies, the debate about norms has shifted from linguistic norms to translational norms (cf. Schäffner, in press), mainly thanks to the influential work by Toury and Hermans.

Linguistic Norms in Translation Studies

When a more systematic study of translation began in the second half of the twentieth century, it was very much influenced by (applied) linguistics. Translation was understood as a linguistic phenomenon, as an operation performed on languages. This operation was seen as a process of transcoding between source language (SL) and target language (TL), as illustrated by the following definition:

> Translation may be defined as follows: the replacement of textual material in one language (SL) by equivalent material in another language (TL). (Catford, 1965: 20)

Any difference between SL and TL that became obvious in a translation was attributed to the differences in the two linguistic systems. Consequently, translation studies was conceived as a linguistic discipline. The precise description of the systematic regularities between signs and combinations of signs in the two languages involved was seen as a precondition for the faithful and accurate reproduction of the source-language text. The target-language text was required to be identical to the SL-text in content, style, and effect, and to respect the rules and norms of the TL. Linguistic translation studies, thus, were basically interested in the norms of the language systems. The linguistic units of SL and TL were compared in order to set up mechanisms (in the sense of normative translation principles) for overcoming differences in the language structures encountered in the process of translation. A translation norm in this context was defined as translating a linguistic unit by its generally accepted equivalent (a position which is still held by some scholars today, as evident in the debates).

A huge number of studies into specific linguistic phenomena provided detailed explanations of regularities in SL and TL, and tried to derive rules, or norms, for translation. Topics that were discussed in journal articles or in books were, for example, how to translate German conditionals into Russian, the substitution of word classes in translation, German pre-nominal extended attributes translated into English (all examples taken from the German translation journal *Fremdsprachen* between 1974 and 1980). The starting point was always a specific linguistic structure or phenomenon in the SL for which methods of translation were provided, as a kind of ready-made solution for the practising translator.

Highly influential in this respect have been the seven methods of translation of the *Stylistique comparée* (Vinay & Darbelnet, 1958), set up on the basis of a comparison of the lexical and syntactic structures of English and French. A similarly practical and pedagogical purpose underlies Newmark's (1988) seven translation procedures, and Friederich's (1969) techniques of translation for the language pair English and German. All these studies are based on a contrastive analysis of linguistic units and syntactic structures which are seen as correct in the two languages.

Friederich's book *Technik des Übersetzens. Englisch und Deutsch*, first published in 1969 and reprinted several times since then (latest edition 1995) can serve as an illustration of the studies that were conducted within this normative linguistic approach. In 25 chapters, Friederich discusses linguistic translation problems and gives techniques (practically in the sense of rules) for dealing with them. The problems he discusses range from lexical issues to syntactic structures, with a specific focus on differences in the linguistic systems of English and German. All chapters are constructed in a fairly similar way: the translation problem is given, and the various possible solutions are illustrated by a large number of examples, which, however, do not go beyond the sentence level. There are no comments about the context or the genre. The focus is on showing the possibilities that are allowed by the linguistic systems. Therefore, Friederich's presentation is often rather general, which becomes obvious in formulations such as 'in the German language we can ...', or 'the English language allows ...'. Such general statements make his translation procedures highly prescriptive.

The concept of norms is important in two respects in linguistic approaches to translation. On the one hand, they are concerned with the linguistic norms of the two languages, i.e. how to produce utterances and texts that are correct according to the respective rules and norms. On the other hand, the relations and regularities between the two linguistic systems that were discovered on the basis of contrastive analyses were 'translated' into guidelines or rules for the translator, mostly with prescriptive intent (cf. frequently encountered formulations such as 'translators must (not) ..., should ...', etc.). Translation procedures and similar guidelines, however, were formulated in a rather general way and gave the impression that they are applicable throughout. A chosen TL-form may well be correct according to the rules of the language system, but this does not necessarily mean that the text as a whole appropriately fulfils its communicative function in the TL-situation and culture. Since we do not translate words or grammatical forms, but texts with a specific communicative function, the limitations of a narrow linguistic approach soon became obvious. Thus, a logical development was that in the 1970s, the insights and approaches of textlinguistics, a new (sub-)discipline of (applied) linguistics, were adopted in translation studies. Thus, regularities of the text itself, of the genre, and of the context were given more consideration.

Norms and Conventions in Text-linguistic Approaches

Textlinguistics defines the text as the basic unit of communication and, therefore, as the primary object of research. For translation studies this means that the text itself is considered to be the unit of translation. Translation is no longer defined as transcoding linguistic signs, but as retextualising the SL-text. The focus has changed from reproducing meanings to producing texts, as illustrated in Neubert's definition of translation as 'source-text induced target-text production' (Neubert, 1985: 18).

The basic assumption of textlinguistic approaches to translation is that SL- and TL-text do not only differ in their sentence structures, which are determined by the respective linguistic systems, but also in regularities beyond the sentence boundaries. In other words, text norms need to be added to the norms of the linguistic systems (Neubert & Shreve, 1992: 22ff.). Based on identified regularities, texts can be categorised into text-types, genres, text-classes. Text-typological, or genre conventions, are culture-specific and can change over time, which makes genres relevant for translation studies. As a result of a systematic comparison and description of genres in SL and TL, prototypes of text types, or genre profiles, can be set up. Such profiles can serve as models for the retextualisation of the SL-text according to the TL conventions. In other words, knowledge of cross-cultural similarities and/or differences in genre conventions is crucial to the translator in order to produce appropriate TL-texts.

In this context, the notion of norms becomes relevant again, in the sense of knowledge of genre regularities, i.e. knowledge of how to produce a text as an exemplar of a genre (or text type) according to the norms. It also involves expectations about the structure of a particular text. With reference to texts and genres, many scholars prefer to speak of conventions instead of norms (e.g. Reiß & Vermeer, 1991: 178), with the argument that norms are usually associated with rules, and non-adherence to them results in sanctions. Conventions, however, are not binding, but only embody preferences.

In recent years, an increasing number of studies have investigated genre conventions, both at macro- and micro-level, from a translational perspective (e.g. Göpferich, 1995, and the contributions in Trosborg, 1997). Genre profiles are useful for translation practice and translator training, but also limited. On the one hand, not all genres are highly conventionalised and, therefore, more readily predictable as to their structure. And on the other hand, a large portion of texts contain both constant and variable elements, which textlinguistic translation studies must be aware of in their attempt to discover text type-specific translation regularities, as Wilss (1996: 21) points out. Hatim and Mason (1997) explicitly include departures from norms into their model text typology. They argue that unmarked texts correspond to the norm, i.e. they operate within the constraints of a recognisable genre. Departures from norms are usually motivated, e.g. by stylistic reasons, and translators need to be able to recognise such deviations and to deal with them (Hatim & Mason, 1997: 54).

The Concept of Equivalence

Both linguistic and text-linguistic approaches are very much concerned with devising optimal methods of translation and with providing guidelines for translators. For both approaches, translation involves a specific relationship between the source (language) text and the target (language) text. This relationship is typically labelled *equivalence*, although there have been several definitions of this notion — where it is not rejected outright (e.g. by Holz-Mänttäri, 1984, cf. also Halverson, 1997).

When the target text is expected to be a faithful reproduction of the source text, then equivalence is defined as identity (of meaning and/or form), not necessarily in the strict sense of interchangeability and complete reversibility, but more often in the sense of equal value or correspondence (cf. Snell-Hornby, 1988: 13ff.). Types of equivalence were suggested in order to specify the relationship between SL-text and TL-text, for example Nida's formal equivalence and dynamic equivalence (Nida, 1964), or Koller's denotative, connotative, text-normative, pragmatic, and formal-aesthetic equivalence (cf. Koller, 1979: 215f). It has been (and still is) argued that translation needs to be set apart from other kinds of derived texts, as reflected in the opposition of translation (proper) and adaptation (e.g. Koller, 1979), semantic translation and communicative translation (Newmark, 1981), overt and covert translation (House, 1977), and that the label 'translation' should be reserved for those cases where an equivalence relation obtains.

There is still much controversy on this point, and this is also apparent in the debates presented in this issue. Functionalist approaches see equivalence as one possible relationship among others (e.g. Reiss & Vermeer, 1991). Descriptive translation studies, of which both Toury and Hermans are representative, see translation as the result of a socially contexted behavioural type of activity (Toury, 1980), or as implying 'a degree of manipulation of the source text for a certain purpose' (Hermans, 1985: 11). Toury shifted the focus of attention by saying that a translation is every text that is regarded and accepted as a translation by a given community. For him, equivalence is only a label that is affixed to a translational relation that is assumed to exist between two texts (Toury, 1980: 39, 65). This reversal of perspective opened the way to a reassessment of the notion of equivalence, since now we can ask for the type of translational relation that exists in a certain case, and for the reasons that one specific type exists and not another. The crucial instrument to help answer these questions is the concept of norms, i.e. translational norms.

Translational Norms

Norms function in a community as standards or models of correct or appropriate behaviour and of correct or appropriate behavioural products. Whereas linguistic and text-linguistic (and also to a certain extent functionalist) approaches focus on the product (i.e. the target text) and on the linguistic norms and genre conventions that determine (the production of) this product, Toury defines norms as being central to the act and the event of translating. Norms are 'a category for descriptive analysis of translation phenomena' (Toury, 1980: 57), or more specifically, norms are 'the translation of general values or ideas shared by a certain community — as to what is right and wrong, adequate and inadequate — into specific performance-instructions appropriate for and applicable to specific situations' (Toury, 1980: 51). Translational behaviour is contextualised as social behaviour, and translational norms are understood as internalised behavioural constraints which embody the values shared by a community. All decisions in the translation process are thus primarily governed by such norms, and not (dominantly or exclusively) by the two language systems involved.

Toury (1980: 53ff.) described three kinds of norms: (1) preliminary norms, which decide the overall translation strategy and the choice of texts to be translated, (2) initial norms, which govern the translator's decision to adhere primarily to the source text or to the target culture, and (3) operational norms, which control the actual decisions made during the act of translation. If it is accepted that norms are central to translating, then their nature and their function need to be explained more systematically. This involves questions such as: how can we establish which particular general concept of translation prevailed in a particular community at a particular time? How does this concept compare to general concepts of translation that were valid at another time and/or in other communities? Who are the norm authorities? Who introduced changes in dominant norms, and why were they accepted? Since translating is situated in time and space, any answer to such questions implies a careful description of the situation and the culture in which such norms obtain. As Halverson (1997: 216) observes, 'the consequence of adopting a norm-based theory of translation is that the object of study for historical-descriptive approaches becomes regularities of translation behavior (norms) and the situational/cultural features which may account for these regularities'.

In the two main contributions to this CILS issue, Toury and Hermans — although opting for different styles of presentation and argumentation — provide examples of translation (or translator's) behaviour which they explain in terms of norms or conventions. In discussing an historical case, Adrianus de Buck's 1653 translation of Boethius, Hermans uses the concept of norms to inquire into the translator's choices. He argues that the choices which a translator makes simultaneously highlight the excluded alternatives, and that in this way light can be shed on the interplay between the translator's responses to expectations, constraints and pressures in a social context. Toury reflects on the expectations about the nature and role of translation within a society, and thus on the expectations about preferred options, by giving as an example three different Hebrew versions of Hemingway's short story 'The Killers'.

Translational norms prevail at a certain period and within a particular society, and they determine the selection, the production and the reception of translations. Based on the work by Toury and Hermans, Chesterman (1993, 1997) differentiates between expectancy norms and professional norms. Expectancy norms refer to what the target language community expects a translation to look like 'regarding grammaticality, acceptability, appropriateness, style, textuality, preferred conventions of form or discourse and the like' (Chesterman, 1993: 17). Professional norms govern the accepted methods and strategies of the translation process, and they can be subdivided into three major types: accountability norms, communication norms, relation norms.

Bartsch (1987: 176) speaks of norms as consisting of two parts: norm content and normative force. The norm content is a socially shared notion of what is correct, and, as Hermans argues in his position paper, norms and conventions are intimately tied up with values. Dominant values in a society reflect the power relationships in that society. This has as a consequence that translation can never be value-free. Translations as cultural and historical phenomena are characterised by opaqueness, and by lack of transparency or neutrality. In contrast to Toury, Hermans argues against retaining the notion of equivalence in our discourse on translation — a problem that formed a substantial part in the debates.

As said above, the notion of equivalence has played an important role in the perception and presentation of translation. Pym (1995) makes a useful distinction between an external view of translation (held by clients, or readers, of translation, who are assuming that translation means sameness) and an internal view (held mainly by translation scholars, who know that translating is much more complex). Because of this complexity, some translation scholars prefer to speak of translation as rewriting, textual manipulation, or appropriation, and they argue that equivalence is not really a broad enough term to cover the kinds of activities that translators do. But exactly how much and what kind of rewriting is prescribed, preferred or allowed in practice, depends on the prevailing concepts of translation. This brings us to the aspect of the normative force, and to the related question of who has the power to enforce norms.

If norms 'act as constraints on behaviour, foreclosing certain options while suggesting others' (Hermans, 1991: 161), they also provide models and guidelines for correct behaviour. As far as linguistic norms are concerned, they are usually codified in an institutionalised way, for example in grammar books and lexicons. In translation studies, scholars have attempted to set up normative translation laws and translation rules or guidelines, typically with a practical purpose in mind (particularly teaching). Such rules are meant both to explain translation regularities and to predict certain structures (thus limiting choices), and typical formats are 'if — then', or 'translators must, should, ought to'. In these contexts, however, 'normative' is meant in the sense of 'prescriptive'. This sense is, unfortunately, also often found in standards or handbooks on translation, cf.:

> The translation should be a faithful rendition of the work into English; it shall neither omit anything from the original text nor add anything to it other than such verbal changes as are necessary in translating into English. (*A Handbook for Literary Translators*, 1991: 16, quoted in Venuti, 1995: 310)

In its sense of 'descriptive' it refers to the study of the norms themselves or to the study of the 'products, processes or behaviour that are taken to constitute or represent norms' (Chesterman, 1993: 11). It is this descriptive sense which is dominant in the two main contributions of this *CILS* issue. The ambiguity of the terms 'norm' and 'normative' is sometimes obvious in the debates, although less so in the responses. The written responses come from scholars who did not attend the meeting, which has made it possible to widen the perspective and add some new ideas.

Describing translation as norm-governed behaviour in a social, cultural, and historical situation, raises a number of issues. For example, how do we get from the norms to the text, and how do we reconstruct norms from textual features? What is the relationship between regular patterns in texts and norms? How do translators acquire norms, do they behave according to norms, and are they conscious of their norm-governed behaviour? What happens if translators show some kind of deviant behaviour? Are translators themselves powerful enough to introduce and change norms? Are there translation specific norms, or more general norms in society that also influence translational behaviour? What can sociological theories contribute to an understanding of norms? Do norms really exist, as social facts, or are they just hypotheses? Is the behaviour of translators indeed governed by norms, or are they rather actively involved in the maintenance of norms (cf. Simeoni's habitus-governed account, Simeoni, 1998).

These are some of the questions raised and discussed in the two main contributions, in the debates and in the responses. Some have not (yet) been answered in full; some will continue to provoke controversy. New questions will undoubtedly emerge as a result of our academic interest in translational phenomena.

References

Bartsch, R. (1987) *Norms of Language*. London: Longman.

Catford, J.C. (1965) *A Linguistic Theory of Translation. An Essay in Applied Linguistics*. London: Oxford University Press.

Chesterman, A. (1993) From 'is' to 'ought': Laws, norms and strategies in translation studies. *Target* 5, 1–20.

Chesterman, A. (1997) *Memes of Translation: The Spread of Ideas in Translation Theory*. Amsterdam and Philadelphia: Benjamins.

Friederich, W. (1969) *Technik des Übersetzens. Englisch und Deutsch*. Munich: Hueber.

Göpferich, S. (1995) *Textsorten in Naturwissenschaft und Technik. Pragmatische Typologie — Kontrastierung — Translation*. Tübingen: Narr.

Halverson, S. (1997) The concept of equivalence in translation studies: Much ado about something. *Target* 9, 207–33.

Hatim, B. and Mason, I. (1997) *The Translator as Communicator*. London: Routledge.

Hermans, T. (ed.) (1985) *The Manipulation of Literature: Studies in Literary Translation*. London: Croom Helm.

Hermans, T. (1991) Translational norms and correct translations. In K.M. van Leuven-Zwart and T. Naaijkens (eds) *Translation Studies: The State of the Art* (pp. 155–69). Amsterdam: Rodopi.

Holz-Mänttäri, J. (1984) *Translatorisches Handeln. Theorie und Methode*. Helsinki: Suomalainen Tiedeakatemia.

House, J. (1977) *A Model for Translation Quality Assessment*. Tübingen: Narr.

Koller, W. (1979) *Einführung in die Übersetzungswissenschaft*. Heidelberg: Quelle & Meyer.

Neubert, A. (1985) *Text and Translation*. Leipzig: Enzyklopädie.

Neubert, A. and Shreve, G. (1992) *Translation as Text*. Kent: Kent State University Press.

Newmark, P. (1981) *Approaches to Translation*. Oxford: Pergamon.

Newmark, P. (1988) *A Textbook of Translation*. London: Prentice Hall.

Nida, E. (1964) *Toward a Science of Translating: With Special Reference to Principles and Procedures Involved in Bible Translating*. Leiden: E.J. Brill.

Pym, A. (1995) European translation studies, une science qui derange, and why equivalence needn't be a dirty word. *TTR* 8, 153–76.

Reiß, K. and Vermeer, H.J. (^{2}1991) *Grundlegung einer allgemeinen Translationstheorie*. Tübingen: Niemeyer.

Schäffner, C. (in press) Sprach- und Textnormen als Übersetzungsproblem aus sprachwissenschaftlicher Sicht. In A.P. Frank *et al.* (eds) *Übersetzung — Translation — Traduction. An International Handbook of Translation Studies*. Berlin: de Gruyter.

Simeoni, D. (1998) The pivotal status of the translator's habitus. *Target* 10, 1–39.

Snell-Hornby, M. (1988) *Translation Studies. An Integrated Approach*. Amsterdam and Philadelphia: Benjamins.

Toury, G. (1980) *In Search of a Theory of Translation*. Tel Aviv: The Porter Institute for Poetics and Semiotics.

Toury, G. (1995) *Descriptive Translation Studies and Beyond*. Amsterdam and Philadelphia: Benjamins.

Trosborg, A. (ed.) (1997) *Text Typology and Translation*. Amsterdam and Philadelphia: Benjamins.

Vinay, J.-P. and Darbelnet, J. (1958) *Stylistique comparée du français et de l'anglais. Méthode de traduction*. Paris: Didier.

Venuti L. (1995) *The Translator's Invisibility*. London: Routledge.

Wilss, W (1996) *Knowledge and Skills in Translator Behavior*. Amsterdam and Philadelphia: Benjamins.

A Handful of Paragraphs on 'Translation' and 'Norms'

Gideon Toury
The M. Bernstein Chair of Translation Theory, Tel Aviv University, Tel Aviv 69 978, Israel

The format of paragraphs has been chosen to present questions and a few tentative answers on the theme of translation and norms. The formulation of questions is an important aspect of any research programme, and it has been the basis for descriptive-explanatory research as well. Translating as an act and as an event is characterised by variability, it is historically, socially and culturally determined, in short, norm-governed. In the paragraphs below, the following issues are discussed: the relationships between social agreements, conventions, and norms; translational norms, acts of translation and translation events, norms and values, norms for translated texts vs. norms for non-translated texts, competing norms. Comments on the reactions to three different Hebrew translations of Hemingway's short story 'The Killers' are presented at the end of the paper.

1 An Introductory Note on Aims and Strategy of Presentation[1]

This text should not be regarded as a full-fledged paper which offers a well-rounded presentation of all that may be invoked by the two title notions and their possible combinations. The main aim of the text is to supply food for thought for anyone wishing to get into the right mood and prepare for the Aston Seminar on 'Translation and Norms'. Above all, it is meant to lay down some ground rules for an open discussion.

As experts on diet know only too well, food is much more digestible when served in small, well-dosed quantities. It is also much more appetising that way. It is this kind of strategy that was adopted for the present document, and for the very same purposes. Thus, my humble aim is to supply a cocktail (shaken, not stirred) of select questions with a number of tentative answers and an odd (more general) hypothesis. The document should therefore be seen as no more than a series of paragraphs on the theme of our seminar; a (hopefully) coherent whole with a minimum amount of cohesive devices, mainly a number of cross-references, which should allow for a multi-directional kind of reading. I trust this would be acceptable just the same, in view of the fact that, especially in the UK, the notion of 'paragraph' has gained considerable circulation and a measure of respectability as a mode of presenting ideas on translation.

In a way, this is a tribute to Peter Newmark, then, who invented the genre of 'Paragraphs on Translation'. However, as experts on multilingualism and language transfer would surely appreciate, at the root of my thinking in terms of paragraphs there was also contemporary colloquial Hebrew, where *tšmá kéta* (literally: 'listen to a paragraph/segment' but actually something like 'wanna hear something weird/funny') is a common discourse organiser; a marker of *opening*, setting the tone for a rather *casual* mode of presentation (Maschler, in press), which is only too fitting for the aims and strategy of my presentation.

Let me make the terms of reference of my position paper as clear as possible:

as always, my main interest lies with *descriptive-explanatory research* rather than mere theorising. For me, theory formation within Translation Studies has never been an end in itself. Its object has always been to lay a sound basis and supply an elaborate frame of reference for controllable studies into actual behaviour and its results, and the ultimate test of theory is its capacity to do that service.

Moreover, I consider the formulation of *questions* an important aspect (and phase) of any research programme. Therefore I truly believe it is questions we should be focusing on in our seminar rather than any answers that may or may not be suggested, this document included. At the same time, I hope we'll be starting our negotiations with one agreement at least; namely, that the association of 'translation' and 'norms' is not just *valid*, from the theoretical point of view, but of potential *value* too, for whatever each one of us may be interested in doing within Translation Studies; otherwise why take up this topic in the first place? As will soon become clear, my choice of the word 'negotiations', in this connection, is all but rhetorical.

In order to keep a minimum amount of order in this progression of paragraphs, topics for possible discussion will be presented in two separate clusters: a general one, tackling the notions of agreement, convention and norm within a social setting, followed by a more specific cluster, where the same notions will be taken up again and tied to translational behaviour. Some methodological points will also be made where appropriate. Whatever is related to these topic-areas will follow a second introductory section of a *historical* nature, an attempt to supply some contextualising facts to the use of the notion of norms in Translation Studies in the last few decades. Those who find this section too long or too personal are advised to skip it and move directly to paragraph-cluster 3. I feel obliged to do it this way in view of the many distortions in the way recent developments in the discipline have been presented, most notably in Gentzler (1993), which seems to have become a standard work, in this respect.

2 Historical Observations on the Association of 'Norms' and 'Translation'

Let's agree to refrain from going into the question of who was the first to say what. Due to our incomplete knowledge of the history of our own discipline, where the wheel has been and is still being re-invented time and again, such questions are bound to generate hot debates; which is not bad in itself, had it not been for the fact that such debates would inevitably lead us way off track. Personally, I am more than willing to waive all claims for originality of thinking and give up any credit one might like to give me for having been the first to tackle translation as the norm-governed behaviour it tends to be; credit which I never claimed anyway.

Thus, it goes without saying that it wasn't I who suggested the association of 'translation' and 'norms'. This association was very much present, if only implicitly, in the work of Jiří Levý, (1969 [1963]) and James S Holmes (1988), with whom I have always felt the strongest affinity, as well as a number of other scholars. All of these could easily have carried their research well into the realm of translational norms because the foundations were certainly there. Needless to say, they all had predecessors of their own, which would have made it possible

— and not uninteresting — to trace the association of 'translation' and 'norms' further back.

All this notwithstanding, I am probably the one person who would have to take the responsibility — the blame, some will no doubt insist — for having injected the heaviest dose of norms into the veins of Translation Studies in the 1970s and early 1980s, in as much as the substance thus injected indeed dissolved into the bloodstream of the discipline (which is one thing I hope to see verified during our seminar). At the very least I would have to be granted with having made 'norms' a kind of legal tender in the discussion of translation practices and their results; because there have surely been quite a number who have adopted the term as little more than a catch-phrase. That is, without reflecting on any of the necessary consequences, or even trying to find out what those consequences might have been.

For me, the beginning was over 25 years ago, when I started researching for my PhD dissertation; and the notion of norms first presented itself as a means of elegantly bridging a gap I encountered while trying to account for the observed results of translational behaviour during a limited period of time (the crucial years between 1930 and 1945) in the history of translation of one text type, prose fiction, within one culture/language: the Hebrew one.

The gap I am referring to was between the notion of translation as it had come to be used by the beginning of the 1970s and the principles of establishing a corpus for a descriptive-explanatory study such as the one I had in mind. The main problem was how to draw a justifiable, non-arbitrary line between that which would be included in the corpus because it pertains to translation as conceived of by the culture in question, and that which would be left outside of it because it does not. The necessary demarcation could simply not be worked out on the basis of any of the conceptualisations I was able to lay my hands on, and for quite a while I became a fervent collector of definitions of translation, in the wild hope of hitting upon the ultimate one.

I soon realised that my difficulties stemmed from the very nature of the essentialistic definition, imposing as it does a deductive mode of reasoning, rather than the formulation of any single definition. Even the most flexible of these definitions, as long as it still purported to list the necessary and sufficient conditions for an entity to be regarded as translational, proved to be unworkable. It then dawned on me that, in the very attempt to define translation, there was an untenable pretence of fixing once and for all the boundaries of a category which is characterised precisely by its *variability*: difference across cultures, variation within a culture and change over time. Not only was the field of study thus offered considerably shrunk, in comparison with what cultures had been and were still willing to accept as translational, but research limited to such pre-defined boundaries could not help but breed a circular kind of reasoning: to the extent that the definition is taken seriously, whatever is tackled — selected for study because it is known to fall within its domain — is bound to reaffirm it; and if, for one reason or another, it is then found to be at odds with the initial definition, it will have to be banished from the corpus. In extreme cases, when actual behaviour is in little congruence with the definition, there would remain hardly anything to study as translations, which is inconsistent with presystematic intuitions based on our acquaintance with the history of translation.

The way out of that deadlock seemed to me to try and have variability in all its facets *introduced into the notion of translation itself*, whereby any kind of realisation of that notion would necessarily be regarded as historically, socially and culturally determined; in brief, as norm-governed.

Needless to say, any attempt to close the gap in any real manner necessitated a lot more than the mere introduction of a WORD such as 'norm' into the theoretical arsenal (in which Itamar Even-Zohar's 1971 seminal PhD dissertation was of paramount importance, in my particular case). It had to be made *operable*. I therefore invested time and effort in theoretical and methodological elaborations on the NOTION of norm, especially in relation to its possible application to translation.

The results came into the open during the pioneering Conference on Literature and Translation, which was held in Leuven (Belgium) in 1976 (for the Proceedings see Holmes *et al.*, 1978) — my first international conference ever. Unfortunately, it was only the skeletal English version (Toury, 1978) rather than the full Hebrew text (Toury, 1977) which became available, and that version was quite correctly characterised as overly schematic; a reflection of its having been a mere summary. In fact, schematism proved to be the strength of that paper as well as its weakness, making it appealing to some and repellent to others, even to this very day. It worked particularly well when regarded alongside Even-Zohar's presentation to the same Conference, entitled 'The Position of Translated Literature within the Literary Polysystem' (Even-Zohar, 1978). Unfortunately, the close connections between the two were all too soon forgotten, which was no great help to the appropriate reception of my first paper on norms.

Unlike the development in recent years, conferences on translation, especially truly scholarly ones, were quite rare in the 1970s. Even against this backdrop, the Leuven Meeting was a unique event: with very few exceptions, it brought together a non-randomly selected group of relatively young scholars, many of them graduate students like myself. I therefore found myself preaching to people who were basically on the verge of conversion to a sociocultural way of thinking about translation anyway. Many of them had, in fact, crossed the critical threshold and were ready for more. This is probably the sense in which my partner in the present Seminar, Theo Hermans (who was among the participants of the Leuven Conference himself), later claimed that time was ripe for a change of paradigms of this precise nature and that translation scholars were well prepared for one brand or another of systemic reasoning which has the notion of norms built into it (Hermans, 1995). Unfortunately, while this might have been true for the group convening in Leuven and their disciples, it hardly held for Translation Studies as a whole. I have already expressed my wonder as to the extent to which it holds today...

At the beginning of the 1980s, a number of colleagues, especially younger ones, adopted the notion of norms and tried to apply it to their own corpora, trying to solve the problems they themselves were keen on solving. Some of them even developed the notion itself in different ways, or at least criticised the simplicity and rigidity of my skeletal presentation, making me rethink it in more and more *dynamic* terms. Due to their personal backgrounds, most of the scholars who tried their hands with the notion of norm were first and foremost engaged in the study of literary translation. However, while this focused interest is easy enough to explain, it is not the case that literature is the only domain where translation can be expected to be norm-governed. It is simply that the notion of the norm has hardly been put to a serious test as an explanatory tool in any other field. This, in other words, is a weakness of Translation Studies in the present phase of its evolution and of its proponents as individuals, rather than of the notion of the norm itself, which has much wider, maybe even universal applicability (see first attempts to apply the notion to Conference Interpreting, of all modes of translation; most notably in Shlesinger, 1989 and Harris, 1990. To judge from recent conferences, these attempts will soon be revived.)

This marks our transition to the cluster of paragraphs, beginning with the more general ones.

3 Social Agreements, Conventions and Norms

Norm-hunting, in any domain of human behaviour, clearly indicates that a sociocultural perspective was opted for. To the extent that such a perspective can be justified, there is no escape from taking seriously what the Social Sciences have to offer us. We need not become sociologists ourselves to do so. In our case, we can still wish to solve the specific riddles of translation, but we would be doing so on the assumption that translation is basically a sociocultural, and hence norm-governed activity (see paragraph 4.1). In the following paragraphs, a selection of sociocultural notions will be presented, in a way which would pave the way for their subsequent association with translation.

3.1 Agreements and conventions

An important assumption of sociologists and social anthropologists is that there must be some humanly innate flair for socialising, which some have named *sociability*. This faculty is assumed to be activated whenever a number of persons come into contact and start exploring their situation with a view to living together. They do this whether what is at stake is the establishment of a new group or just the sustenance of an existing one. As J. Davis — an anthropologist who tried to systematise the notion of 'social creativity' and render it serviceable in explaining the making and maintenance of social groups — recently put it:

> People use their given sociability to create *agreements about actions*. So, our worlds achieve the appearance *of stability and regularity* because we agree that certain actions are acceptable in appropriate circumstances, and others are not. (Davis, 1994: 97, italics added)

Rather than given, (tacit or explicit) 'agreements about actions' are always *negotiated*, with or without the intervention of language. Such negotiations, which require some time, result in the establishment of social *conventions*, according to which members of the group will behave when they find themselves under particular circumstances. They often do so in the form of behavioural *routines*. 'What we create is — within agreed limits — a predictable event, from which certain choices have been excluded'. 'So when we are [socially] creative we attempt to create order and predictability and to eliminate choice, or at any rate to confine choice within certain prescribed limits' (Davis, 1994: 97).

3.2 Negotiations and re-negotiations

In as much as a group is indeed formed, or its existence sustained, the process involving negotiations, agreements and conventions-and-routines can thus be regarded as inevitable. The exact way it proceeds in any individual case, by contrast, is not given in any way. Rather, it is a function of the prevailing circumstances. Many times it may even seem as if 'it could so easily have been otherwise' (Davis, 1994: 97). At the same time, in retrospect, what was opted for can normally be accounted for; the agreements themselves as well as the way they were negotiated and reached.

Nor is the establishment of a societal group merely a time-consuming process. In addition to its gradual nature it is also a never-ending one: as long as the group has not collapsed, social order and everything that goes with it are constantly being (re-)negotiated; the more so when new members wish to join the group or when it is challenged by rivalling groups. Small wonder, then, that the process also involves adjustments, and hence changes, of agreements, conventions and behavioural routines. In fact, the most one would get is temporary, sometimes — i.e. in very unstable societies — even momentary states of equilibrium.

3.3 Conventions and norms

Conventions are a necessary outcome of any striving for social order, as well as a means for its attainment and maintenance. At the same time, they are not specific and binding enough to serve as guidelines for (and/or a mechanism for the assessment of) instances of behaviour and their products. Due to their inherent vagueness, the acquisition of conventions poses special problems to newcomers to a group, which would be the normal case with new translators starting to work in and for an established society (paragraph 4.11). There is a 'missing link' here which the notion of norm seems a good candidate for supplying.

3.4 Norms

Norms have long been regarded as the translation of general values or ideas shared by a group — as to what is conventionally right and wrong, adequate and inadequate — into performance instructions appropriate for and applicable to particular situations, specifying what is prescribed and forbidden, as well as what is tolerated and permitted in a certain behavioural dimension (the famous 'square of normativity', which has recently been elaborated on with specific regard to translation, e.g. in De Geest, 1992: 38–40). They do so even if one refuses to accept that values act as causal elements of culture, as a sort of ultimate ends towards which action is directed, and maintains instead that

> culture influences action not by providing the ultimate values toward which action is oriented, but by shaping a repertoire or 'tool kit' of habits, skills, and styles from which people construct 'strategies of action'. (Swidler, 1986: 273)

As long as there is such a thing as appropriate vs. inappropriate behaviour (according to an underlying set of agreements), there will be a need for performance instructions as well. In a way, then, norms may be seen as part of Swidler's 'tool kit': while they may not be 'strategies of action' in themselves, they certainly give rise — and lend justification — to such strategies.

3.5 Norms vs. normative formulations

Not only can social negotiations be carried out with or without the intervention of language (paragraph 3.1), but also the norms themselves which would govern behaviour need not be formulated at all: They may well remain implicit. At the same time, there is always at least the *possibility* of having norms verbalised, in order simply to comment on them (or on norm-governed behaviour and its results) or even as part of the process of imparting them to others to ensure social continuity.

This possibility notwithstanding, it is important to bear in mind that there is no identity between the norms as the guidelines, as which they act, and any formulation given to them in language. Verbalisations obviously reflect *awareness* of the existence of norms and their significance. However, they always embody other interests too, particularly a desire to *control* behaviour — i.e. dictate norms (e.g. by culture planners) — or *account* for them in a conscious, systematic way (e.g. by scholars). Normative formulations may, therefore, serve as a source of data on norm-governed behaviour, and hence on the underlying norms as such, but they may do so only indirectly: if one wishes to expose the bare norms, any given formulation will have to be stripped of the alien interests it has accumulated.

3.6 Norms and regularities of behaviour

Obviously, there is a point in assuming the existence of norms only in situations which allow for alternative kinds of behaviour, involving the need to select among these, with the additional condition that selection be non-random. In as much as a norm is active and effective, one can therefore distinguish regularity of behaviour in recurrent situations of the same type, which is the clearest manifestation of the 'order and predictability' Davis (1994: 97) regards as characteristic of social creativity (see paragraph 3.1).

Needless to say, whatever regularities are observed, they themselves are not the norms. They are only external evidence of the latter's activity, from which the norms themselves (that is, the 'instructions' which yielded those regularities) are still to be extracted; whether by scholars wishing to get to the bottom of a norm-governed behaviour or by persons wishing to be accepted in the group and hence needing to undergo socialisation (paragraph 3.7).

There is an interesting reversal of direction here: whereas in actual practice, it is subjugation to norms that breeds norm-governed behaviour which then results in regularities of surface realisations, the search for norms within any scholarly programme must proceed the other way around. Thus, it is regularities in the observable results of a particular kind of behaviour, assumed to have been governed by norms, which are first noted. Only then does one go on to extract the norms themselves, on the (not all that straightforward) assumption that observed regularities testify to recurrent underlying motives, and in a direct manner, at that. For the researcher norms thus emerge as *explanatory hypotheses* (of observed [results of] behaviour) rather than entities in their own right.

3.7 Norms and sanctions

In an established group, norms are basically acquired by the individual — a newcomer to the group on whatever grounds — in the process of his/her socialisation (paragraph 3.6). Very often, these norms — or even the basic agreements and conventions — go on being negotiated throughout one's entire life in the group, for instance, when members struggle to establish their own positions within the group (or *vis-à-vis* its other members). Moreover, certain individuals may be more instrumental than others in effecting changes in the norms, depending on the status and position they have acquired in the group.

Be that as it may, unlike the weaker, more obscure conventions (paragraph 3.3), the notion of norms always implies *sanctions*; actual or at least potential, whether negative (to those who violate them) or positive (to those who abide by them). Within the group, norms also serve as a yardstick according to which instances of behaviour and/or their results are evaluated, the second, complementary role any kind of norms is designed to fulfil.

3.8 The graded and relative nature of norms

The instruction-like constraints of the norm type are far from monolithic: not only are some of them more binding than others, at any single point in time, but their validity and relative strength are bound to change over time.

Firstly, in terms of their *potency*, constraints on behaviour can be described along a scale anchored between two extremes: general, relatively absolute rules on the one hand, and pure idiosyncrasies on the other. The vast ground between the two extremes is occupied by norms, which, in turn, form a graded continuum: some are more rule-like, others — almost idiosyncratic. In fact, we — members of a group as well as observers from without, including researchers — can recognise a mode of behaviour or its results as being idiosyncratic (or inevitable, for that matter) only against the backdrop of our acquaintance with the middle ground and its internal gradation. Nor is the centrality of norms metaphoric only, in terms of their relative position along a posited continuum. In a very strong sense, the other two types of constraints are mere variations of norms, and not independent entities. Consequently, they may easily — and justifiably — be redefined in their terms: rules as '[more] objective', idiosyncrasies as '[more] subjective [or: less inter-subjective]' norms.

Secondly, the borderlines between the various types of constraints are diffuse. Each of the concepts, including the grading itself, is relative too, depending on the point of view from which they are regarded, or the context into which they are entered. Thus, what is just a favoured mode of behaviour within a large and/or heterogeneous group may well be assigned much more binding force within a particular subgroup thereof, which is likely to be more homogeneous too (e.g. translators among text-producers, translators of literature among translators, translators of poetry among translators of literature, translators active in a systemic centre vs. translators who operate on a periphery, etc.). A similar kind of relativity can be discerned in terms of types of activity, forming either parts of each other (e.g. interpreting, or legal translation, within translation at large) or just sharing adjacent territories (e.g. translation criticism vs. actual translation [paragraph 4.9]). Thus, even if it is one and the same person who engages in more than one activity, and/or belongs to more than one (sub)group, s/he may well abide by different norms, and manifest different kinds of behaviour, in each one of his/her roles and social contexts. The ability to manoeuvre between alternative sets of norms is of course an important aspect of social life, and its acquisition is an important component of socialisation.

Thirdly, along the *temporal* axis, each type of constraint may and often does move into its neighbouring domain(s) through processes of rise and decline. Thus, under certain circumstances (which would have to be specified), mere whims may catch on and become more and more binding, and norms can gain so much validity that, for all practical purposes, they become as strong as rules. This may also happen the other way around, of course: what used to be binding may lose much of its force, what used to be common may become rare, what was once common to many may become idiosyncratic, on occasion even bizarre. Needless to say, what was taken up in basically synchronic terms under the second point can also be projected on the diachronic axis, which compounds the possibilities as well as the difficulties inherent in the scholarly hunt for norms.

3.9 Norms and power relations

As already indicated (paragraph 3.7), shifts of validity and potency have a lot to do with changes of status, and hence with power relations; whether these occur within the group itself or whether power is imposed on it from without (a claim which — when stripped of its ideological overtones — is far from an innovation of postmodernist, feminist, post-colonialist and suchlike approaches to society and culture). Whatever these shifts, they can always be accounted for in connection with the notion of norm, especially since, in as much as the process goes on and social agreements are re-negotiated, the constraints are likely to cross its realm (paragraph 3.8), i.e. actually *become* norms, at least for the time being.

Having covered some general ground, let us move on to tying the notions of social agreements, conventions and (especially) norms to the particular kind of behaviour which translation appears to be.

4 Norms of Translation

4.1 Does translation carry the notion of 'norm'?

It has often been claimed that every act of translation involves a unique encounter of an individual with a text within a specific communication situation. Does such a view of translation carry the notion of 'norm' at all?

'The scope of sociability covers all our activities', says Davis (1994: 97); and translation is certainly an activity which is of sociocultural relevance.

> We try to do all these things in a conventional way, and when we agree that we have options we try to create conventional ways of deciding among them. And you should note that creative activity is continuous: [conventionalised kinds of behaviour] would cease to happen if we did not, so to

speak, renew the understanding which makes them, each time [...]. (Davis, 1994: 97)

In fact, it is not difficult to see why translation should lend itself to treatment in terms of sociability, and quite easily so. After all, it is basically performed within a sociocultural context, more often than not for the consumption of persons other than the producers of the translated texts themselves, who may be said to form some kind of a group together (paragraph 4.4). While there does exist the notion of socially-insignificant translation (i.e. individuals translating for themselves, so to speak; e.g. Harris & Sherwood, 1978), its practice is surely negligible. Moreover — and more importantly, in this context — most socially-redundant instances of translation can be expected to simulate socially-relevant ones anyway, wittingly or unwittingly. Consequently, norms are bound to affect them too, and the same norms, at that (which is one important way how *potential* sanctions may be said to be taken into account [paragraph 3.7]).

4.2 Acts of translation vs. translation events

But is translation not a cognitive process? Does it take place anywhere else except in an individual's brain? And if this is the case, what could the explanatory power of sociocultural notions such as conventions and norms possibly be? Should acts of translation not be accounted for in purely *mental* terms? Should we not all turn to the cognitive sciences, if what we are interested in finding out is what translation activities consist of and how they proceed in 'real life'?

True enough. All translation decisions are made in an individual's brain. At the same time, positing an incongruity, let alone contradiction, between the cognitive and the sociocultural seems a gross exaggeration, especially in the context of translation; an incongruity which diminishes to the point of losing its pointed tip as soon as a distinction is drawn between the *act of translation*, which is indeed cognitive, and the context of situation where the person performing the act, and hence the act itself, are embedded, which has sometimes (e.g. Toury, 1995: 249ff.) been called the *translation event*.

Needless to say, no translation event can be said to have taken place unless an act of translation was indeed performed. On the other hand, at least in socially-relevant instances of translation, including simulated ones (paragraph 4.1), all cognitive processes occur within contexts which constitute events. This much I believe should be taken for granted, and it should be justification enough for approaching the overall event in sociocultural terms.

One thing I would not venture to do here is tackle the intriguing question of how, and to what extent, the environment affects the workings of the brain, or how the cognitive is influenced by the sociocultural, even though this would surely make an invaluable contribution to our understanding of translation (see, in this connection, recent attempts to use the notion of 'meme' in Translation Studies, especially to account for changes in the concept of translation itself and the way they travel; most notably in Vermeer, 1997 and Chesterman, 1997.) We will return to the possible influence of the environment on translation performance in the more specific context of socialisation; in this case — the emergence of an individual translator within an established sociocultural setting (paragraph 4.11).

4.3 'All is predestined — but freedom of choice is granted'

But is the concept of norm, especially in its application to translators, and hence its association with translational behaviour, not too rigid, as many seem to maintain? Is it really the case that acceptance of the idea that translation events are basically norm-governed entails the denial of free choice during an act of translation which is embedded in it? — Not at all! To borrow a concept from traditional Jewish thinking: 'All is predestined but freedom of choice is granted' (*Avot* [The Sayings of the Fathers], 3: 15).

To put it bluntly, it is always the translator herself or himself, as an autonomous individual, who decides how to behave, be that decision fully conscious or not. Whatever the degree of awareness, it is s/he who will also have to bear the consequences. Remember the notion of sanctions (paragraph 3.7)? At the same time, it is clear that, even though there is always the possibility that one would be willing to take the risks which unconventional, non-normative decisions entail, under normal conditions, a translator would tend to avoid negative sanctions on 'improper' behaviour as much as obtain the rewards which go with a 'proper' one. Needless to say, it would make an interesting project to study the [negative and positive] sanctions that may be associated with translational behaviour and their (possible and actual) effects on instances of performance within defined sociocultural settings (see the way Daniel Simeoni has recently related the concept of 'norm' and Bourdieu's notion of 'habitus' in the specific context of translation, Simeoni, 1998).

In fact, translators have even been known to act differently, or at least to produce different surface realisations of the category 'translation' (i.e. differently looking utterances), when working for different commissioners, e.g. in order to be given more work by the same commissioners, or at least to escape the need to have their products edited by others, which many translators abhor. To be sure, freedom of choice is exerted not only when one chooses to behave in a way which does *not* concur with the prevailing norms. It is also exercised when one seems simply to reaffirm one's previous commitment to these. After all, in principle, there is always an alternative, otherwise there would be no need for norms in the first place (paragraph 3.6).

4.4 What group is it where agreements are negotiated?

If agreements and conventions are constantly being negotiated (paragraph 3.2), and if norms are one of their outcomes and modes of implementation in actual behaviour (paragraph 3.3), it would only be proper to enquire as to where those negotiations take place, in the case of translation; in other words, what constitutes 'the group' in question. For instance,

- How homogeneous (or heterogeneous) should that group be taken to be?
- Would it always consist of members of the same categories?
- More specifically, would it include acting translators only (which would yield a very limited group indeed), or persons playing other, adjacent roles as well; whether in the production of translations itself (e.g. editors [of translations, or even texts in general]; teachers, especially of translation; translation critics; censors; publishers) or around it?
- And what about (average or specific) consumers of translated utterances:

would they be taken to form part of the group too? And, if so, would it not mean going way too far with the notion of 'group'?

- In a heterogeneous group, how powerful are the translators themselves, with respect to the creation, negotiation, maintenance and change of translational norms? Do they occupy the centre or a peripheral position?
- And what about individuals who play several roles alternately? Is it all that certain that they would act according to exactly the same norms while assuming their different positions?

This is an intriguing domain about which translation scholars seem to know precious little, beyond a small number of accounts of isolated individual cases. There seem to be many alternative patterns here. Thus, there may be larger and smaller groups involved in the negotiations, more or less closely-knit or diffuse, more or less homogeneous, more rigid in their (personal or sectorial) composition, etc. It is not totally unjustified to assume that these differences would manifest themselves as significant, in their implications for translation behaviour and the norms governing it. However, this is about all I would say, at this point (see again Simeoni, 1998).

4.5 The 'value' behind translation

Translation is a kind of activity which inevitably confronts different languages and cultural traditions, and hence different conventions and norms on each pertinent level. Thus, the value behind it, or the basic tools in a translator's 'tool kit', for those who refuse to accept that values behave as causal elements of culture (paragraph 3.4), may be described as consisting of two major elements; namely, producing a text in a certain (so-called 'target') language,

(1) which is designed to occupy a certain position, or fill in a certain slot, in the culture that uses that language while, at the same time,
(2) constituting a representation in that language/culture of another, preexisting text in some other language, belonging to some other culture and occupying a definable position within it.

It is clear that these two types of requirement derive from two sources which — even though the actual discrepancy between them may vary greatly — should be regarded as different in principle. Often they are incompatible in practice too, so that any attempt to abide by the one requires a price in terms of the other, which breeds an inherent need for *compromise*.

4.6 Norms and efficacy

The inevitable compromise between the constraints drawing on the two different sources, while always realised by an individual, is strongly affected by sociocultural factors which determine its appropriateness; the behaviour by the enveloping circumstances, the act by the event. Among other things, this can be seen as a strong factor of *efficacy*.

Thus, were it not for the regulative capacity of norms, the tensions between the two sources of constraints, and hence between adequacy and acceptability (as a translation or as a target-language text) would have to be resolved on an entirely *ad hoc* basis, and with no clear yardstick to go by. Indiscriminate, totally free variation might have been the result, which would have made it next to impossible to locate an act of translation and/or its results within their social context and assign them any cultural relevance. Everything may well have been seen as equal to everything else, which is most certainly never the case; not even in the most permissive of societies. Not even if the ideology appears to be there.

4.7 Regularities of behaviour again

In fact, as any cursory look will ascertain, translation as practised within a particular culture, or a certain sector thereof, tends to manifest quite a number of *regularities*, in terms of both translational adequacy and acceptability (as well as their preferred blends), a fact which we have already taken as strong evidence of the *potency* of norms (paragraph 3.8). On the other hand, these regularities may well differ from the ones exhibited by another culture, cultural sector, or even the same culture in another phase of its evolution (which amount to the same thing, theoretically speaking).

One consequence of the existence of such regularities and their acknowledgment is that, even if they are unable to account for them, people-in-the-culture can at least tell when a translator has failed to adhere to sanctioned practices. For instance, they may not be able to *say* that a certain phenomenon in a translated text reflects interference from the source text/language, but they will at least have a hunch as to what they are expected to *feel* about it, within the preferences of their culture. Different cultures have been known to have had different thresholds of tolerance of interference. Some of them even preferred to have them in translated texts; e.g. in the translation of 'Works of Wisdom' (in contradistinction to the translation of 'Works of Beauty') into Hebrew in the Middle Ages (see Toury, 1998).

4.8 How regular would 'regularities' need to be?

'Regularities' thus turn out to be a key notion in descriptive studies into translational behaviour and its results as well. In fact, the establishment of recurrent patterns is the most basic activity in the pre-explanatory phases of a study, the phases where data are collected and analysed and discoveries are being made. Also, it is first and foremost discerned regularities, rather than any of the individual phenomena as such, which would then be explained on the assumption that the behaviour which yielded them was indeed norm-governed (paragraph 3.6), all the more so as not every observed phenomenon will be subsumable under one of the emerging recurrent patterns in the first place. The beauty of human behaviour, whether under cognitive or sociocultural observation, is that there is no 100 per cent regularity, not even in the behaviour of one person while translating one text, which concurs with the graded and relative nature of the notion of norms (paragraph 3.8). Complete absence of any regularities should also be regarded as marginal: if one looks hard enough (or extends one's corpus enough), reflections of any possible mode of behaviour are sure to be found.

What may seem more frustrating than failure to come up with any absolute findings (which both 'never' and 'always' imply) is that, very often, regularities will first manifest themselves in rather low percentages. Consequently, it will not be all that clear just how much significance should be assigned to each observed regularity. The main reason is that it is almost as hard to establish sampling rules for translational behaviour, or even its textual-linguistic results, as it is to take 'everything' into account. Justifying the status of a body of material as a 'sample' in terms of Translation Studies is even harder.

In actual fact, what a researcher often starts out with is a rather arbitrary set rather than a proper corpus; a group of texts, or a number of lower-level phenomena, which may be both accidental, from a translational point of view, and highly heterogeneous (i.e. devoid of clear regular patterns). The way to go from here is to try and break the initial set into sub-groups on the basis of one feature (variable) or another which will have emerged as significant (for that set) during the study itself. This procedure is bound to yield a substantial increase of homogeneity, reducing each sub-group's accidentality and gradually rendering it representative in terms of that particular variable; in other words, a proper corpus. Within such sub-groups, regularities are bound to increase, often considerably. If found to be too small now, any subgroup-turned-corpus could then be expanded; this time on the basis of the defining feature itself, and hence in a much more justified (and justifiable) fashion.

4.9 Are translational norms translation-specific?

Due to their contending sources (paragraph 4.5), there is no way that the norms governing translation in their totality (that is, the overall 'normative model' a translation event is subject to) will be identical to the ones operating in any other field, be it even a closely-related one. One may of course expect correlations, including partial overlaps, but never full identity. Norms can also be imported from one type of behaviour to another (always with some [necessary] modifications), but the value of each one of these norms is likely to be different due to its different systemic position. The same holds for norms imported from a different group engaging in the same kind of activity, within the same culture and society or in different ones.

Let us look at three types of activity which are closely related to translation: communication in non-translated utterances, translation assessment and translator training.

Type one: *Communication in translated vs. non-translated utterances*. Here, partial overlap is to be expected, as a translation is always an intended utterance in the target language and culture: one aspect (or phase) of any act of translation involves formulation in that language, and the norms governing this activity may of course be more or less similar to the norms governing the composition of a non-translated utterance, and more or less different from them. At the same time, since translation is not reducible to that aspect/phase alone, only partial overlap can be expected.

Overlap between the norms governing translation and non-translation can be expected to grow in direct proportion to the centrality of target-language 'normality' in translation, which is of course a norm-governed idea. 'Acceptability as a translation' may thus become a variety of 'acceptability' in general, which would normally imply reduced interest in the principles governing the source text (or the internal 'web of relationships' which constitutes it) and their reconstruction.

Conversely, imitations of textual-linguistic behaviour in another culture/language (or of certain types of translation from it) may be attempted in non-translational communication as well. The resulting texts may thus bear close resemblance to translations without there ever having been an identifiable source text. This option has often been selected by the creators of so-called 'fictitious translations' (e.g. Toury, 1995: 40–52), precisely in order to convey the impression that those texts had in fact been translated, i.e. lead the people-in-the-culture astray on the basis of what they have come to associate with 'genuine' translations.

Whether the one extreme or the other (and both of them are extremes!), the likely result is a blurring of the borderline between translations and non-translations: all texts would tend to look alike, and whatever differences there may be, it won't be easy to attribute them to the translation/non-translation opposition. On occasions, such an opposition may be found out to have been completely non-functional in the culture in question: even if it is retained on the level of the acts whereby texts are generated, translations may still be presented — and accepted — as originals, and originals as translations, without this having any cultural repercussions.

Such seems to have been the case in the early Enlightenment period in Hebrew literature (Toury, 1995: 131ff.). People-in-the-culture, producers and consumers alike, did not really care which texts were based on foreign ones in a one-to-one manner and which texts were based on them in a one-to-many ratio, or even just embodying the principles of the models underlying particular text-types. Today's scholars face a great many difficulties in ascertaining which one is which, but, in an important sense, they may be trying to solve riddles of very little historical significance, if that is what they are doing.

Type two: *Translation vs. translation assessment.* These two activities differ in a different sense: with respect to the translational product, the one activity is *prospective,* the other one is *retrospective.* Even if both result in textual entities, their end-products are of a different order too: translations are the result of a direct application of translational norms whereas assessments employ first and foremost norms of evaluation and of evaluation-presentation, including the norms governing the composition of evaluative texts. As regards translational norms, evaluators just react to them and their results. Sometimes they may try to extract them from the results of translational behaviour, to a certain extent even verbalise them. What they never do is *implement* the norms, unless they wish to offer an alternative translation (which may be a strategy of critics, even teachers, whereby they change for some time their role, and hence the kind of activity they are engaging in).

Basically, translation and evaluation are two different activities, then, whose governing principles can simply never be 'the same'. What they can do is reflect the same overall *attitude* towards translation, each in its own domain. In this sense, translators and evaluators may belong to the same group (paragraph 4.4). However, even this is not a theoretical must, nor does it always occur in practice. Thus, critics and translators may, and often do have *different* values, e.g. they may favour different blends of acceptability and adequacy; on occasion, even if translation and criticism are performed by one and the same person.

To give an example: whether (or under what circumstances) a translator would feel obliged to read the source text in its entirety before s/he embarks on its translation is a basic strategic decision which may rely more or less on social factors, that is, be norm-governed; be it directly (e.g. there exists an 'instruction' to do precisely that) or indirectly (e.g. through a marked dominance of an initial norm of translation adequacy). Now, whereas every translator who has finished translating will have been through the source text at least once, many translation evaluators, including critics writing on literary translations, or members of committees awarding translation prizes, may never feel an urge to even peep into the original, let alone read it in its entirety. What is most significant here is not simply that this happens, but that a societal group may *accept* it, sometimes even *prefer* it that way.

Type three: *Translation vs. translator training*. This may well be the trickiest comparison. One would think that persons who have been entrusted by society with the training of translators at an accelerated pace, would see their task as imparting modes of behaviour to the non-initiated the way they are normally practised, thus preparing them for acceptance in and by the relevant group (paragraph 4.4). However, this is often not the case. What many students of translation are actually being offered draws on an admixture of concepts borrowed from sources deemed more 'respectable' than the behaviour of real translators under normal sociocultural conditions; mainly disciplines such as linguistics, text-linguistics or pragmatics. These concepts are supplemented by intuitions, sometimes very good ones, but all too often seasoned with a speck of wishful thinking. In the most extreme cases, the claim is even made (at least implicitly) that there are things that simply should be (or else should never be) done; by virtue of what translation allegedly 'is', and not by virtue of a sheer convention; in fact, not seldom in contrast to existing conventions and the agreements which underlie them.

There is normally an ideology behind such attitudes, and ideologies tend to involve a manipulation of existing normative patterns. Thus, many teachers of translation see it as their task to effect changes in the world at large, wishing, as it were, to take active part in the process of (re-)negotiation which is constantly going on (paragraph 3.2). They would of course claim that the prevailing situation is badly in need of improvement, but this would not affect the basic claim that what they are trying to do is *change* a state of affairs, and one which others, including the group of practising translators, may well regard as perfectly satisfactory. They do what they do from a position of almost absolute power (*vis-à-vis* their students), power which was granted to them by the institutions in which they work; sometimes, though not always, and certainly not necessarily, on the basis of their own recognition by society as translators (see, in this connection, Chesterman's 'professional norms', Chesterman, 1993). However, the edge teachers have over their students does not necessarily imply similar position and power within society at large; not even in the 'translatorial' group, whoever it may consist of.

It is possible to say that training institutes often behave like closed groups, having conventions and norms of their own. They are trying to impart these norms to newcomers to this closed group and through them and their future translational activity — to society as a whole. Unfortunately, transition from such a group into the 'world' may not always be all that smooth. In extreme cases it may involve real pain and frustration. Thus, it has not infrequently been the case that the graduates of a translation programme had to undergo a process of forgetting a great deal of what they had been taught and adjusting, at least in part, to prevalent norms of sociocultural appropriateness; very often the very same norms their teachers wished to see changed.

4.10 But are all translations 'good'?

Are teachers of translation (or critics, for that matter) all that wrong? Has everything become so relative that there is no such thing as a bad translation any more? Of course there is, even though there is definitely nothing objective or absolute about that notion either. Rather, notions of what would constitute a bad translation (or a good one, for that matter) are as changing as the notion of translation itself. In fact, judged by our (irrelevant) norms, even the ones we apply to the case of the translation of religious texts, the King James Version of the Bible is surely not a very good translation. From today's point of view, its centrality can only be explained in historical terms. Acknowledging its 'inherent' qualities as both an English text and a translation into English would require the adoption of another attitude, associated with a completely different set of norms, those that were at play at a different point of time and hence in another culture.

The basic thing one must be ready to accept is that bad translations are first and foremost translations, not something completely different. Consequently, whether an item which would be conceived of as a translation is 'good' or 'bad' will be determined by an extension (or further specification) of the normative model pertinent to the culture where it came into being (or the appropriate section within it). It is not that members of a societal group cannot arrive at a valid conclusion in an intuitive way; it is that, if and when required to account for their attitude, they will have to draw on that set of norms — or else be unable to justify their intuitive verdict.

Thus, any attempt to impart the way 'good' translations are (to be) done, e.g. by teachers of translation (paragraph 4.9), may backfire; namely, when society refuses to accept that those are indeed good. Significantly enough, it is often the case that even teachers in one and the same institute, or critics within one culture, do not assess a translation the same way. Differences of assessment, again, may look idiosyncratic, a matter of personal taste and temperament, and to a certain extent this is precisely what they are. However, to an even greater extent they are a result, or a reflection of the affiliation of different persons to different (sub)groups, and to that extent they are a function of norms again. (For the possibility of having different, even competing norms within one and the same group see paragraphs 4.12 and 4.13.)

4.11 How does an individual acquire translational norms?

In modern times, many translators (but still a minority) are indeed being trained, even conditioned, in professional or academic training institutes. We have just touched upon their possible fate (paragraph 4.9). Others, probably the vast majority, pick up the conventions and norms pertinent to their job through a process of initiation within the culture itself, a specific mode of socialisation (paragraphs 3.6–3.7). In view of the lack of any real longitudinal studies into the making of translators outside of the schooling system, the only way to sketch this process is speculative; namely, on the basis of what we know about socialisation in general, with the addition of some translation-specific considerations. The present writer also made use of his insights as to how he himself became a translator back in the 1960s; namely, before he ever did any Translation Studies.

Firstly, if the internalisation of norms is really that important an aspect of translational behaviour, then the acquisition of that knowledge, and of ways of coping with it in real-life situations, should count as a major aspect of socialisation in relation to translating. My assumption here is that, being a mode of communication, translating is likely to involve *environmental feedback*, which may come from any other party to the communication event. This feedback is normative in its very essence: it concerns the well-formedness of a translation, not just as an utterance in the receptor language and culture, but first and foremost as an assumed translation (Toury, 1995: 31–35), that is, a realisation in the culture and language in question of the mode of text-production translating is taken to be. At least by implication, the norms embodied in that feedback also apply to the (minimal, optimal, necessary, etc.) relationships between assumedly translated utterances and their assumed sources, especially in terms of whatever should have remained invariant. By extension, they also determine the appropri- ateness of the strategies used to derive a translational output from a given input utterance under those conditions of invariance, even though there can be no one-to-one relation between a procedure and the results of its application.

Secondly, it is the all-pervasiveness of sanctions (paragraph 3.7) which lends such normative feedback its influence on a translator's behaviour. Under normal conditions, one would wish to avoid negative sanctions on 'improper' behaviour as much as obtain the rewards which go with a 'proper' one (paragraph 4.3). This aspiration holds especially for the novice, who — due to lack of sufficient experience — is likely to feel insecure as to what translating is all about, according to the conception of the group in and for which s/he will be operating, and who, on the other hand, may be looking for recognition by that group in his/her capacity as a (socially-relevant) translator. It is precisely this view which gradually crystallises for her/him in a process of initiation. It may, of course, prove irrelevant again, if and when that person moves to another group, especially if the new group forms part of a completely different culture. Under such circumstances, another process of socialisation may be required.

Thirdly, in the initial stages of one's development as a translator, the feedback directed at him/her is exclusively *external*: overt responses to one's translational products, final or interim. A novice simply has no means of assessing the appropriateness of various options and/or of the alternative strategies that may yield them. Little by little, however, translators may start taking potential responses into account too. They thus develop an *internal* kind of monitoring mechanism, which can operate on the (interim) product as well as on the act of translation as such.

Fourthly, as socialisation in relation to translating goes on, parts of the normatively-motivated feedback are probably assimilated by the translators as they gather more and more experience, modifying their basic (i.e. innate) competence and gradually becoming part of it. Many decisions will now be made more or less *automatically*. It may also be hypothesised that, to the extent that a norm has been internalised and made part of a modified competence, it will be applied to instances of more spontaneous translation too, namely in situations where no sanctions are likely to be imposed. It is in this sense that socially-insignificant instances of translation may be said to simulate socially-significant ones (paragraph 4.1). Some translators may then go on to take active part in the re-negotiations concerning translational conventions (paragraph 3.2) which will sometimes result in a change of norms.

4.12 Alternative norms within a group

One thing which makes translational decision-making less demanding than it may have sounded so far in terms of the risks taken, even though probably more complex in terms of its underlying mechanisms, is the fact that, at every point in the life of a societal group, especially a comprehensive and/or heterogeneous one, there tends to be more than one norm with respect to any behavioural dimension. Consequently, the need to choose between alternative modes of behaviour tends to be built into the very system, so that socialisation as concerns translating often includes acquisition of the ability to manoeuvre efficiently between the alternatives (paragraph 4.6).

Multiplicity of norms does not amount to no norms at all, much less imply anarchy. For it is normally not the case that all existing norms are of an equal status, so that choice between them would be totally free, or devoid of any implications for the assessment of the person's behaviour and/or his/her position within society. Manoeuvring between alternative modes of behaviour thus turns out to be just another norm-governed activity, necessarily involving risks of its own.

4.13 Competing norms

Norms operating within one and the same group are not merely different from each other. Quite often they are competing too. After all, in the dynamic structure of a living society, there is always a struggle for domination, as a result of which norms may change their position *vis-à-vis* a certain centre of gravity, the more so as the centre itself may be undergoing shifts.

What complicates matters even more is the fact that each group-within-a-group (and all groups tend to be hierarchically organised) may have its own structure of centre vs. periphery, entailing an internal struggle for domination of its own, in addition to (and sometimes as part of) its participation in the overall struggle. Consequently, one has to be as clear as possible as to whether one is talking about changes *of* (sub)systems or changes *within* one of them.

Firstly, there is *variation within a culture*. Whether within one (sub)system or between the various (sub)systems regarded as building up one higher-order entity, it is not rare to find side by side three types of competing norms, each having its own followers and a position of its own: the ones that dominate the centre, and hence direct translational behaviour of what is recognised as the *mainstream*, alongside the remnants of *previous* sets of norms and the rudiments of what may eventually become *new* ones, hovering in the periphery (and/or near the centre of lower-order (sub)systems). This is why it is possible to speak — and not derogatorily either — of being 'trendy', 'old-fashioned' or 'progressive' in translation as it is in any other behavioural domain.

Secondly, there are *changes over time*. One's status as a translator, in terms of the norms one adheres to, may of course be temporary: many translators fail to adjust to the changing requirements, or do so to an extent which is deemed insufficient. Thus, as changes of norms occur, formerly progressive translators may soon find themselves just trendy, on occasion even downright *passé*.

At the same time, regarding this process as involving a mere alternation of generations can be misleading, especially if generations are equated with age groups. While there often are correlations between one's position along the 'dated'-'mainstream'-'avant-garde' axis and one's age, these cannot, and should not be taken as inevitable, much less as a starting point for the study of 'norms in action'. As already maintained, there is nothing deterministic here.

In fact, research shows that it is often people who are in the *early* phases of their initiation as translators, whether young or not so young of age, who behave in the most epigonic way. Insecure as most of them understandably are, they like to play it safe and tend to perform according to dated, but still valid norms. One way to explain this is to realise that a beginner's deviant behaviour would more readily be regarded by society as 'erroneous' rather than 'innovative': while both may be applied to the same mode of behaviour (or its products), the different *values* assigned to them make all the difference in the world!

Such a conservative tendency is further enhanced if would-be translators receive reinforcement from socialisation agents, especially powerful ones, holding to dated norms themselves. No wonder that revolutions — i.e. large-scale changes of paradigm — have often been made by *experienced* translators who had, moreover, attained considerable prestige by behaving 'appropriately', i.e. according to mainstream norms. After they internalised those norms, and having attained more than mere recognition by society, they can afford to start deviating from them and get away with it.

4.14 Constraints, strategies and norms

There is another pair of notions which deserves a lot more attention than it has received so far, namely that of 'strategy' and 'norm'. Let us regard as a strategy any set of moves utilised in trying to solve a perceived problem; perceived by the one performing the act, that is.

Intuitively, there seems to be some connection between strategies, on the one hand, and norms on the other. However, the nature of that connection has not been clarified; probably mainly due to the fact that those who focused on translation strategies (e.g. Wolfgang Lörscher, 1991) have normally considered mere *acts of translation* rather than *translation events* (paragraph 4.2) whereas most socioculturally-oriented scholars have not followed the progression from the event to the act. I believe it is about time that we had both ends meet, if only for the purpose of supplying better, more comprehensive and more flexible explanations of the translational behaviour of individuals within a societal context (and see Simeoni, 1998 once again). Such explanations are also bound to assign a third notion, that of constraints, its proper place in the account of translation rather than its mere 'opening conditions'.

5 By Way of Conclusion: A Story of Three 'Killers'

Let me conclude with one of my favourite cases, which may be taken as a nut-shell exemplification of many of the points made throughout this document.

In the last few decades, three different Hebrew translations of Hemingway's famous short story 'The Killers' were published, at almost identical intervals, and not very long ones, at that: the first translation (A) was published in 1955, the second one (B) in 1973 and the third and last one (C) in 1988. Linguistically, each one of the three textual entities is of course different, which is all but surprising; the more so as every translator seems to have been aware of the earlier version(s). In fact, some of the decisions made by later translators could be taken as indications of so-called 'polemical translation'; see Popovič, 1976: 21.)

What is most interesting, however, and not all that evident, is that when asked to put the three translations in their correct chronological order, everybody — from complete newcomers to thinking about translation to experienced transla-tors, teachers of translation and translation scholars — came up with precisely the same order. Moreover, with very few cases of local disagreement, when asked to justify their ordering, they all based it on the same series of features; basically an assortment of semantic, grammatical, syntactic, pragmatic and stylistic markers, as well as translation relationships, which the subjects seem to have associated with 'typical behaviour' of literary translators into Hebrew at the three different points in time (or at least of its gradual change along time).

Now, the significant thing is that, in spite of a 100 per cent agreement between dozens of subjects who have undergone this pseudo-experiment, they were all wrong: the order they came up with — which was based on their intuitive-to-learned ability to identify relevant markers and associate them with modes of translation (and, yes, the norms which governed them) — that order did not conform to reality. Thus, the order they all gave was ACB instead of ABC.

When I disclosed the names of the translators (actually, four of them, because the 1973 version (B) was prepared by two persons jointly), there were quite a number of subjects who were able to correct their initial ordering. The names acted as additional information for them, because they had cultural knowledge as to who was more or less likely to count as 'dated', 'mainstream' or 'avant-garde' in their translational behaviour.

Finally, once all subjects learnt of their factual error, it was relatively easy to explain to them how, historically rather than chronologically speaking (that is, in terms of the appropriate norms and their position in society), they had not been all that wrong, after all. Thus, only one of the three translations was appropriate for the time at which it was produced and the expectations of its intended consumers, namely, the first one (A). The other two versions were either ahead of their time (B) or somewhat obsolete (C); two kinds of deviation from 'mainstream norms' which were automatically 'corrected' by all readers.

The bottom line seems clear enough: not only are there norms associated with translation, but people-in-the-culture know how to, and actually do activate them; not only while producing translations themselves but while consuming them as well. What is still unclear is whether production- and consumption-norms are exactly the same, even in this individual case, i.e. which group it is that generates and negotiates translational norms, but we have already presented this as a moot point (paragraph 4.4).

Note

1. I have decided to have the paper published in a format almost identical to that which served as basis for the seminar, i.e. with only minor amendments. The reason behind this decision is to let the readers see how I tried to stimulate the debate.

References

Chesterman, A. (1993) From 'is' to 'ought': Laws, norms and strategies in translation studies. *Target* 5, 1–20.

Chesterman, A. (1997) *Memes of Translation*. Amsterdam and Philadelphia: Benjamins.

Davis, J. (1994) Social creativity. In C.M. Hann (ed.) *When History Accelerates: Essays on Rapid Social Change, Complexity and Creativity* (pp. 95–110). London and Atlantic Highlands, NJ: The Athlone Press.

Even-Zohar, I. (1971) Introduction to a theory of literary translation. Unpublished PhD thesis (in Hebrew), Tel Aviv University.

Even-Zohar, I. (1978) The position of translated literature within the literary polysystem. In J.S Holmes *et al.* (eds) *Literature and Translation: New Perspectives in Literary Studies* (pp. 117–27) . Leuven: Acco. (Revised version in Even-Zohar, 1990: 45–51.)

Even-Zohar, I. (1990) *Polysystem Studies*. Tel Aviv: The Porter Institute for Poetics and Semiotics, and Durham: Duke University Press (*Poetics Today* 11:1).

Geest, D. De (1992) The notion of 'system': Its theoretical importance and its methodological implications for a functionalist translation theory. In H. Kittel (ed.) *Geschichte, System, Literarische Übersetzung/Histories, Systems, Literary Translations* (pp. 32–45). Berlin: Erich Schmidt.

Gentzler, E. (1993) *Contemporary Translation Theories*. London and New York: Routledge.

Harris, B. (1990) Norms in interpretation. *Target* 2, 115–19.

Harris, B. and Sherwood, B. (1978) Translating as an innate skill. In D. Gerver and S.H. Wallace (eds) *Language, Interpretation and Communication* (pp. 155–70). New York and London: Plenum.

Hermans, T. (1991) Translational norms and correct translations. In K.M. van Leuven-Zwart and T. Naaijkens (eds) *Translation Studies: The State of the Art. Proceedings of the First James S Holmes Symposium on Translation Studies* (pp. 155–69). Amsterdam and Atlanta, GA: Rodopi.

Hermans, T. (1995) Toury's empiricism version one. *The Translator* 1, 215–23.

Holmes, J.S (1988) *Translated! Papers on Literary Translation and Translation Studies*. Amsterdam: Rodopi.

Holmes, J.S, Lambert, J. and van den Broeck, R. (eds) (1978) *Literature and Translation: New Perspectives in Literary Studies*. Leuven: Acco.

Levý, J. (1969, 1963) *Die literarische Übersetzung: Theorie einer Kunstgattung* (Walter Schamschula, trans.) Frankfurt am Main and Bonn: Athenäum.

Lörscher, W. (1991) *Translation Performance, Translation Process, and Translation Strategies*. Tübingen: Narr.

Maschler, Y. (in press) Rotsè lishmoa kéta? ('wanna hear something weird/funny [lit. 'a segment']?'): The discourse markers segmenting Israeli Hebrew talk-in-interaction. In A. Jucker and Y. Ziv (eds) *Discourse Markers*. Amsterdam and Philadelphia: Benjamins.

Popovič, A. (1976) *Dictionary for the Analysis of Literary Translation*. Edmonton: The University of Alberta, Department of Comparative Literature; Nitra: The Pedagogical Faculty, Department of Literary Communication.

Shlesinger, M. (1989) Extending the theory of translation to interpretation: Norms as a case in Point. *Target* 1, 111–15.

Simeoni, D. (1998) The pivotal status of the translator's habitus. *Target* 10, 1–39.

Swidler, A. (1986) Culture in action: Symbols and strategies. *American Sociological Review* 51, 273–86.

Toury, G. (1977) *Translational Norms and Literary Translation into Hebrew, 1930–1945* (in Hebrew). Tel Aviv: The Porter Institute for Poetics and Semiotics, Tel Aviv University.

Toury, G. (1978) The nature and role of norms in literary translation. In J.S Holmes *et al.* (eds) *Literature and Translation: New Perspectives in Literary Studies* (pp. 83–100). Leuven: Acco. (Revised version in Toury, 1995: 53–69.)

Toury, G. (1995) *Descriptive Translation Studies and Beyond*. Amsterdam and Philadelphia: Benjamins.

Toury, G. (1998) Hebrew tradition. In M. Baker (ed.) *Encyclopedia of Translation Studies* (pp. 439–48). London: Routledge.

Vermeer, H.J. (1997) Translation and the 'meme'. *Target* 9, 155–66.

The First Debate

The Meaning of *Hamlet* and Poems

Peter Newmark (Surrey University): Gideon said that translation is always changing and what was considered to be a translation some years ago would not be recognised as one today. I think that it would. I myself think that a translation basically remains the same. There is a bit too much of talk about avant-garde norms, or old-fashioned and reactionary ideas in your position paper. I do not recognise such terms in translation. I do recognise norms, but I think norms are in many ways superficial compared with the more permanent elements of a text.

Gideon Toury (Tel Aviv University): I am sorry, but I must disagree, partly because I have been working on translation within a tradition where the differences are much more marked, because everything took place at an accelerated pace. For example, at the end of my position paper, there is the story of 'The Killers', by Ernest Hemingway. The difference in time between the three translations was something like 15 years, and in spite of the very short distance in terms of time, it was very easy for almost every native speaker of Hebrew to locate them correctly. Only, as it turned out, they were not correctly located. The translations were done in different ways, one of them in the normal way for its time, the other proved to be an avant-garde translation. It was not an avant-garde one to start with, it was simply different, deviant. They could not know in the 1970s that 15 years later this would be the way that the average translator would work. The third one was simply dated. But all these ways do not have any one common denominator, they have nothing in common. I think you and I are interested in two different aspects; although we would both agree that there is a common denominator which you can find in the texts over time, or even across cultures, but there are also differences, many of which would be due to different norms. You would be more inclined to focus on that which the texts have in common, whereas I would be more interested in the differences and the sources of these differences.

Peter Newmark: If I get a translation of, let's say *Hamlet*, I want to know how close it is to what *Hamlet* means. That is what I am looking for. I am not interested in whether it is avant-garde or not. I would expect it to be written in the modern language, hopefully, although there are exceptions even to that.

Theo Hermans (University College London): I think that there is no clear answer to the question what *Hamlet* might possibly mean. Let me refer to an essay by Stanley Fish about Blake's poem 'Tiger, Tiger, burning bright'. The poem consists of a number of questions which the reader can answer with either 'yes' or 'no'. Which answer you choose depends on how you read the words, on what value you attribute to the words in the text. For example the word 'forest', does it mean a positive and good natural habitat or does it mean hostile environment? So what a reader construes as the meaning of the text is not fixed and stable but it depends on where s/he comes from. We cannot read *Hamlet* in the same way as a reader in the nineteenth century did. The French do not read *Hamlet* in the same way as the Russians, and even the English text is not stable. What *Hamlet* means is what we make of it, or what a community of readers accepts as valid readings at a certain moment.

Peter Newmark: I do not think that 'Tiger, Tiger ...', one of the most wonderful poems in the English language, has been misinterpreted. There are no good or bad connotations in the word 'forest'.

Gideon Toury: But the question is simply: Should we read the poem through the eyes of somebody reading it in 1998 or not?

Peter Newmark: You should simply read poetry as poetry. The eighteenth century was certainly the century of norms, of elevation of style, and celebration of Tytler. However, Blake was against constraints and he was in favour of relaxing, and he was a wonderful poet. The recognition which I get when I read 'Tiger, Tiger ...' is what interests me. The fact that I read it in the late twentieth century and Blake wrote it in the eighteenth century is of no importance.

Peter Bush (The British Centre for Literary Translation, University of East Anglia): If you were going to translate Blake, then it would matter.

Peter Newmark: I don't think it would. I think that one wants to translate Blake into the modern language.

Gideon Toury: That would be a first norm-directed decision that you would make, to translate it into the modern language. Why not translate it into archaic language, or into an artificially archaised kind of language?

Peter Newmark: Because I am not capable of it, and also because it would make my vision of Blake something which is artificial. There are some translations, for example of Dante, where archaic language has been successful, but these are exceptions. A lot of things are according to norms, and a lot of things are not according to norms. I am not trying to make it a rule that all translations should be made into the modern language. There are exceptions, but the translator has to be capable of empathising with the work.

Theo Hermans: The reason why I brought Blake up in the first place, was to try and answer the question about what *Hamlet* means. There is this nice essay which demonstrates that when we interpret Blake, individuals and groups of individuals do not do so randomly. There are readings of Blake which are not regarded as valid by communities. Neither can the meanings that we attribute to a particular poem be unequivocally reduced to the essence of the text. The point of mentioning Blake and the essay by Fish is precisely to suggest that there are interpretive communities within which, at a certain point in time and place, certain readings are accepted as valid, or preferred, and others are not. Interpretation, too, is norm governed.

Bible Translations

Peter Newmark: When I read a poem, or *Hamlet*, or some other text, I want to understand what it means. Or when I, as a teacher, speak about a text with my students, I want to give them an insight into what we are talking about.

Gideon Toury: As an individual person, I am not interested in a text in the same way as I am interested in it when I am doing scholarly work, especially along historical lines. Would you not like, for example, to be able to give your students an insight into why the King James Version of the Bible would be regarded as a terrible translation nowadays?

Peter Newmark: I am surprised by your remark. When you say this, you mean because of a few inaccuracies, presumably. It is wonderfully written and translated, and therefore the reverse of 'terribly bad'. The King James Version of the Bible has been one of the formative influences in the English language.

Gideon Toury: Right, but it was not very well written in terms of the seventeenth century. It became very well written when the English language changed.

Peter Newmark: I wouldn't agree with this. To me, something that is 'well written' is well written whenever it was written. I assume that you are talking simply about the inaccuracies of that version when you say that the King James translation is now considered to be poor.

Gideon Toury: No! It was considered to be good English, but had it been produced today, with the norms that we now hold *vis-à-vis* translating, it would be considered as a very bad translation.

Peter Newmark: But what are your reasons?

Gideon Toury: The reason is that this is not the normal way of doing translations nowadays.

Peter Newmark: Are you talking about the changes in the language?

Gideon Toury: I am talking about what one normally does when one encounters a word which one does not understand. At that time they simply transliterated it for their version of the Bible, and that would not be done today. The conception of translation nowadays does include transliteration, but to a very limited degree, with respect to names etc., but not with respect to a word like 'mammon', for example. We know that there is the word 'mammon' in the King James Version, because the translators simply did not understand what it was. There are dozens of words like this in the Bible, and I think it would be regarded a very deviant kind of solution, had it been used today.

Peter Newmark: But 'mammon' has to be read in its context. It has been incorporated into the English language, meaning wealth, greed, and it is well understood. Many words are transliterated or transferred today.

Gideon Toury: Nobody knows what it means. In modern Hebrew it means 'heaps of money', but this is its meaning in modern Hebrew, it is definitely not biblical.

Beverly Adab (Aston University): Peter, you were talking about getting an insight into what a text means, and that a well-written text means well-written at any time. What are your criteria for evaluating if something is well written? Doesn't the perception of a text as being well-written rely on an understanding of the norms that were valid at the time a text was written?

Peter Newmark: Not with Shakespeare. I consider Shakespeare to be well-written. It expresses thought closely, it expresses the topic closely. It is a concise, accurate, lyrical approach which uses all the resources of language. You are confusing norms with standards. Norms are social and I am trying to produce some kind of individual judgement which other people would consider to be subjective. The Manipulation School relies on what they call descriptive, objective approaches. Well, this is important, but I also think one needs to include subjectivity, and especially when one is talking about literature which is full of imagination and intuition. This is my approach to 'good writing'.

Theo Hermans: Coming back to the Bible translations. I do not agree with what Gideon said, namely that the Authorised Version, had it been written today, would be regarded as a poor translation. I would say that it depends on the context, and on what kind of audience feels itself as being addressed. For example, the French Chouraqui translation, which is even much more literal than the Authorised Version, and also has all the Hebrewisms that the Authorised Version has but to a much greater extreme, is accepted in some circles. Very recently, an English translation along the same lines was published. But, I think, that neither Chouraqui nor this new literalist English translation will ever achieve general acceptability. And this notion of acceptability also answers Peter Newmark's original question about how translation changes. I think the key to that answer could be that there is a difference between periods and communities regarding what certain communities at certain moments accept or do not accept as translations. The best example I can think of is du Bellay's argument in the sixteenth century. He writes that translation, because of its nature, does not allow any room for manoeuvre for the translator, and therefore cannot lead to elegant, eloquent texts. If you wish to import into your culture texts which are eloquent and well-written, then you should not translate. What you should do instead is imitate. To him, 'translation' and 'imitation' are two very different concepts. A hundred years later, also in France, Nicolas Perrot D'Ablancourt does all the things that du Bellay calls 'imitation', and yet he calls them 'translation'. The operations that he performs have not changed. What has changed is that du Bellay would not regard imitation as translation, where as D'Ablancourt encompasses under 'translation' also all those things that a hundred years before were called 'imitation'. So it has to do with what you accept under a certain category or under a certain term.

Paul Chilton (Aston University): There are some interesting points in du Bellay's theory of translation. What he meant by imitation is not completely clear, but some light is shed on it by the fact that he used a metaphor, the metaphor of digestion. He talks about digesting, specifically digesting the vocabulary from Italian literature, as well as Latin, and the point of this is to expand the literary vocabulary of French. The whole endeavour has a political context. In fact, the title of that tract *Défense et illustration de la langue française* is not accidental. It is a defence of French against the prestige of Italian culture and Italian literature. The whole notion of translation and imitation of du Bellay is part of a political project, which is the production of a French national culture as part of a French nation state. So this is one crucial way in which translation can fit into a much broader sociopolitical context. The other point which comes out from du Bellay, is that there is no clear-cut boundary between languages. He regards the boundaries as fluid, realised, for example, in bringing words in in the process of translation. When you translate from one language to another, you actually import all of the morphology and phonology of the source language.

Theo Hermans: I agree. In the text of du Bellay's treatise, the way in which it changes from speaking about translation to talking about 'imitation' is absolutely striking, and the metaphor that you mentioned is crucial in this. He speaks about swallowing, digesting, ingesting the writing of the Italians. This way of speaking about it belongs to a long tradition of writing about imitation, going back to the Romans, and as being distinct from translation. We know exactly what he is talking about and why the two concepts meet, perhaps even overlap to some extent, but are seen as essentially two very different exercises. And yet, when one hundred years later D'Ablancourt is talking about his form of translation and admits that not everybody might be willing to call this translation, he is doing exactly what du Bellay called imitation. They do the same things, but they put very different labels on them.

Historicity and Subjectivity

Peter Bush: Gideon, on the one hand you say that you have an approach which is historicising, and on the other hand you have one which is sociological. This is fine, but actually, I think, the whole idea of 'norm' seems to leave out history. Then you make a distinction between yourself as a scholar and yourself as a reader. This is a convenient division, but I am not sure that it works so easily, because however scientifically objective you would like your scholarship to be, you cannot exclude yourself from your research. If translation is changing, you as a scholar are subjectively analysing that change. There is a dialectical interaction, but you seem to be leaving out the subjectivity. For example, you said that to read eighteenth-century translations, we need to find out about eighteenth-century norms to read them correctly. You could reconstruct what you perceive to be eighteenth-century norms of translation, but that would in no way be an eighteenth-century conception of norms of translation. That would be a reconstruction carried out in the 1990s from your point of view as a scholar of translation.

Gideon Toury: Is there any other way of doing history?

Peter Bush: There is no other way of doing history, but that is why all of that has to be taken into consideration in your theorising. You talk about norms shared by communities, but by which communities? And what does community mean?

Gideon Toury: Well, it is part of the research programme to find out what constitutes a community. For example, when I talk about translation into Hebrew, a tradition I have some knowledge of, I know about the different personalities of translators, what groups they belonged to, I know about the way they argued among themselves, the periodicals they had, what intentions they had, and so on. I am not ignoring that, and I am also not ignoring the subjective part. In order to justify one's decision to do any kind of research, we must be aware of the fact that we cannot neutralise ourselves completely, but that we should also try not to involve too much of our subjectivity into the discussion.

Alexandra Lianeri (Warwick University): If one denies the existence of a universal concept of translation and recognises, as Descriptive Translation Studies do, the multiplicity of conceptions of translation in different cultures, then the employment of a positivistic approach to translation phenomena, which would argue that the language of translation theory can be neutral and purely descriptive, becomes problematic. One cannot simply describe data without imposing or using one's culture and cultural presuppositions. I think that the notion of 'pure' description leads to a self-contradiction as it does not account for the fact that one's scientific definition of translation, which is socially and culturally· specific, would determine one's approach to the historical realities under study. When we speak of a sociologically oriented approach to translation, which view of society do we have? The description of society in terms of systems theory, which assumes that both the formation and change of norms are determined by the need of the system to maintain its viability and coherence, is not a neutral depiction of sociocultural phenomena. I also wonder about the extent to which this view can be reconciled with your argument that norms are also the products of unequal power relations within the target community.

Gideon Toury: You seem to like dichotomies, whereas I always try to compromise because we need to forge tools with which we go about our work. I really do not see a huge opposition between sociology and history, or between studying social groups and the changes that occur within them. I think that nowadays sociology no longer works without a notion of dynamics. And dynamics assumes changes, not only looking at more or less stable or unstable states of affairs at a certain point of time, but also studying changes over time.

Peter Newmark: I think we ought to be talking more about morals and aesthetics than about sociology and anthropology, although these have their place in any translation discussion. But I would like to know whether we are talking about translation of imaginary subjects, that is literature, or about translation of fact, i.e. non-literature. I think in our discussion it is unclear what people are talking about.

Peter Bush: I am not a relativist, nor am I a post-modernist. I believe that texts exist and that authors wrote them, but I also believe that readers interpret them. What I am interested in is the relationship between a text that is historically produced in a particular context and is then read, and whether there is any communality in this experience. I am interested in this from the point of view of a literary translator, as a translator of imaginative fiction. This is why I worry about scholarship that wants to leave out subjectivity because it seems to me that literary translation, like many other forms of translation, is an intensely subjective experience which is historically and socially constructed. A theory of scholarship that wants to analyse that practice but that leaves out its own subjectivity, how would this ever penetrate that subjectivity which it is trying to analyse? Gideon, if you want to leave out subjectivity in your own research, that's fine. But I think we have to find a way for including subjectivity in our research in order to explore other issues which would then also reflect on norms in translation.

Gideon Toury: The question of the deliberate omission of subjectivity is directly related to the use of data in a general context. Many translation scholars are trying to find regularities. You personally are probably more interested in finding irregularities. I could question your approach by saying that you will never know what would count as idiosyncratic or individual unless you know what the general background is. This is a vicious circle for all of us.

Norms and Ethics

Theo Hermans: Earlier, I spoke about interpretation, and that it is norm governed. I think we need to add that it is also acquired, it is learnt. School children and students learn to read texts in certain ways, and this changes over time. This also places an ethical responsibility on the person teaching interpretation, and equally, the person teaching translation does have an ethical responsibility. I do not think that Gideon can deny that what he and Peter Newmark and other translation scholars write about translation does affect the concept of translation that we have. To that extent your hanging on to the notion of objectivity, your desire to stand back from the object of study, is not entirely persuasive to me.

Gideon Toury: Before I started doing translation studies in the early 1970s, I had been translating, and I also indulged in translation criticism. The first thing I decided to drop was my side occupation as a reviewer, and I decided to do so precisely because I came to realise that a review coming from my pen would be read differently than a review from somebody else. I am not unaware of my subjectivity, although I have tried to neutralise it. I think that for society at large, doing translation is much more important and influential than doing translation studies. This is why I still continue doing translation, I want to leave a mark on my own society. And when I do translate in my own society, I am well aware of the times when I break rules and norms. I do it considerately, I take into account the possibility that my translations will not be accepted, or that they will be imitated by others. I am not an unethical person, but I still think that there is a difference between ethics in translation and translation teaching on the one hand, and ethics in translation theory, on the other hand.

Peter Newmark: In my theory of translation, there are five medial factors, and one of them is morals, which I think is important.

Gideon Toury: Yes, but basically in a prospective way of thinking about translation.

Peter Newmark: Of course, for me as a teacher, it is the prospective view of translation, rather than the retrospective view, which most interests me.

Gunilla Anderman (University of Surrey): Gideon, are there times when you wish you had called 'norms' something else? And if you had, do you think we would be having a different type of discussion?

Gideon Toury: No, I don't. There is always a problem when you devise something which is new, even if it is not absolutely new but building on previous ideas. You need words to talk about it. There are two ways to go about this: firstly, you invent your own words, but then you may talk a kind of strange or foreign language, and nobody else understands you. The other way is to use existing words but redefine them. This would seem an easier option, but it involves difficulties of its own. When you read about the new ideas, but you have not really learned the new uses of the word, then you keep reinterpreting what you are reading according to your previous knowledge of these words. This is a delicate issue, and I have not worked out which way is really better. I still think that using existing words makes life easier, although I may be wrong. Theo

Hermans keeps writing that I should drop the use of the word 'equivalence' because I have redefined it. But if I changed the name now it would cause more problems that if I stick to a term and keep reminding the reader that it means something different to what they might expect. As far as the term 'norms' is concerned, I am not sure. I have made selections from various existing approaches to norms, but I don't think I have changed anything myself. I have decided, though, unlike other people, not to regard conventions as very weak norms, but as something else.

Models for Reconstructing Norms

Loredana Polezzi (Warwick University): We have been talking about norms and reconstructing norms, and how to historicise them. I think that the notion of the norm is essentially important because it helps to produce questions. These questions can then be turned into a model, but we can also safely say that we want to historicise these questions. What we have in the end is not an abstract model for reconstructing norms that could work at any time and anywhere, but rather a checklist to help us with our research, a kind of strategy for saying: these are the questions we should be looking at. But we are not trying to make a model out of these, which can be applied without any historical context. Some of these questions may produce very interesting answers in some historical or social circumstances, and some of them may not.

Gideon Toury: I would not say that a model and a checklist are mutually exclusive, although I am not so sure if I understand correctly what you mean by 'model' in this context. But also if you want to formulate questions, this would not mean that you have to go to extremes and say that from now on we have a checklist and we will ask the same questions all over again. I would say that questions are acceptable, but let the corpus dictate or at least direct the asking of the questions. We certainly should not work with a closed checklist. And once you ask questions you are aiming at a model. A 'model' for me, in this context, would be a structure of norms.

Loredana Polezzi: You talked about the aim being to reconstruct norms, and how to go about it. I wonder whether we shouldn't go one step further and say that in the end it is not really the norms that we are interested in, but how a norm was formed, how it has changed, what the position of translation was in this changing of norms, etc. It is really the dynamics of change that we should be interested in. This relates to what Theo was saying earlier about interpretative communities. So we ask what translations do in certain settings and how they function for the people who receive them. And the answers will be different, depending on the community and the time. When we look at what translations do, we also need to ask how the translation was produced and what the intention was. Whatever the translator did at that time, whether it was constructing a French literature or not, can we take it as intentionalised? And as a translation moves through history, is it doing the same thing, or is the same translation used to do something completely different?

Gideon Toury: I would certainly agree that we do not wish to end up with just a formulation of norms. We should also ask additional questions such as 'why do translators stick to certain norms and not to others? Where were they imported from? What happened later on?' I cannot say if this involves intentionality, because I am working in a different terminological set where intentionality is alien. I would have to reinterpret the term in some way if I wanted to include it. And even though I have been working with the notion of norm for 25 years, I would not pretend to have all the answers to the questions I myself ask. There are probably many questions I have never even asked! I do not see anything wrong with this. In one of my articles I called translation studies an 'optimistic discipline' because there is always some new question to address. And I do research into translation because it is a fascinating issue.

Theo Hermans: When you say that you should let the corpus generate the questions, you are putting the cart before the horse. Even the constitution of your corpus is governed by a particular model. There is always a theory first of all, which directs the attention, otherwise you would not be able to see anything at all. Of course you are adapting as you go along, but it is your searchlight which illuminates certain things and obscures others. The relevance of studying norms historically would be that you do not do it for its own sake. It is not the norms or the construction of the norms in themselves that matters, but ultimately it is how people handle norms. Why do certain norms apply and not others? What strategies do people develop to handle these norms? And you do that in order to study cultural history, the cultural relevance of translations. You would ask questions like why did certain translations matter or why not? What difference did they make in society, why did they bring about which changes? All our constructions in these terms, about what we regard as the significance of a certain translation, or what kind of norm complexes appear to be relevant, are only constructions, not reconstructions.

Defining (Types of) Norms

Paul Chilton: One of the things that strikes me, as an outsider to the area of translation studies, is the fact that the discussion of norms and whether there are absolute criteria for something called 'good writing' is taking place at all. These questions have been discussed in other social sciences for a long time. It seems to me to be self-evident that norms of some kind are operating, in translation as an area of human behaviour as in others. What troubles me is that it hasn't really been made clear what is meant by 'norm' as it has been used here. I am particularly interested in the idea of 'ethical norms' and how these may enter into translation. There seem to be other ideas of 'norm' around, for example norm almost in the sense of an etiquette, or prescription as to what is considered acceptable in a society in a given period. What I would like to contribute are my own reflections on my own practice as a translator, and specifically as a translator of a sixteenth- century French text, *L'Heptaméron*, by a woman writer, Marguerite de Navarre. In doing this translation and reflecting on it, norms have entered into the process. For example, when I approached this translation, I had to look at earlier translations. It was clear from nineteenth-century translations that the text had been bowdlerised. The original text was a collection of immodest stories, and the Victorian translators had censored it. There are two issues here. The first is that they were operating an ethical norm, that is, they cut out everything that was not ethically acceptable . The second issue is whether the translator has a right to alter the content of the source text in the first place. Now, because of the culture and the time I lived in and because of the norms under which I was operating, I felt that I did not have the right to cut out any passages at all in the original text, whether I disapproved of them or not.

Peter Newmark: And this is an ethical decision.

Paul Chilton: Precisely. In a sense, I was no better than the Victorians, since I was constructing my own, ethically influenced, version of the source text. This was conscious: I was aware of norms operating — ethical norms in a developing society in the late twentieth century that I, as a translator, was subject to. Translation and interpretation go hand in hand here. Marguerite de Navarre's text is nowadays regarded as an early feminist text. My focus as a translator was on those features of gender conflict and gender issues within the dialogues in that text. In some ways I was sensitised by the linguistic choice that I made as a translator to bringing these issues out. I was conscious of it, I was affected by the ethical norms of the society I was living in. A further area concerned literary genre, style and fashion. The source text has a number of passages in verse, and I had to take the decision whether to translate those into verse. They were written in archaic French, so I had to take the decision of whether to reflect that in some way. I did decide to translate into verse, but this does not seem to me to be an ethical decision at all, but purely a stylistic one which has to do with literary expectations that one believes one's contemporary readers might have. To sum up, I was conscious of ethical and non-ethical norms. I think that perhaps we need to be more precise and that we need to sub-classify more clearly the type of norms that enter into the translation process.

Gideon Toury: I do not think that there are differences between the norms, but there are differences in terms of the domains that the norms apply to. They operate very similarly, whatever the domain is, whether they are stylistic or ethical norms. I am not sure that stylistic norms are any different from ethical norms, I think ethical considerations are also involved in stylistic decisions. What I find most interesting in your presentation is that the decisions that you had to make do not seem all that automatic. They were induced by something. For example, you said that you 'had to look at earlier translations'. Where does the 'had to' come from? Is there an absolute rule that someone who is translating a text which has already been translated before 'has to' look at previous translations in order to see what other translators did?

Paul Chilton: I think that the fact that I looked at the previous translations is not specific to translation as such. It simply arose from some sort of norm of scholarship in general.

Gideon Toury: Some of the other points you mentioned have been widely discussed in translation studies, so I'm not going into detail. But I would like to take up one other thing you wondered about, namely whether poetic passages should be translated into verse or prose. In my culture, this question would hardly have arisen at all, because the norm has been, for the last 250 years, to translate verse by verse. In fact, with us, sometimes the question is whether passages in a text which are not in verse should not actually be rendered in verse.

All decisions a translator takes are individual decisions, but they are made in a historical and social context, and there are already precedences for how to deal with a certain problem.

Gunilla Anderman: To me, norms explain certain things in translation, which until I viewed it along those lines, remained a bit of a mystery. For example, the biographer of both Strindberg and Ibsen very happily declared that Ibsen is a very good writer, but Strindberg is a less good writer. It is only if you compare the existing literary norms in the Anglo-Saxon tradition with the norms within which Ibsen and Strindberg wrote, that you realise that Ibsen was much closer to the literary norm in Anglo-Saxon culture. You then understand why whatever the translator does, some translations would be branded as 'bad'. And this has much to do with the difference of the existing norms. I get the feeling that in our discussion, norms are associated with prescriptiveness. The more I listen, the more I hear about what one 'shouldn't' do and 'should' do. I have looked at norms as a means to provide an explanation of certain phenomena, also in a historical perspective.

Gideon Toury: I think, assuming that if the norms actually existed, they had some power to compel people to either abide by them, or if they do not abide by them, they would be willing to pay the price.

Christina Schäffner (Aston University): This is related to the question of 'consciousness'. Are you aware of norms, or has somebody told you how to translate, how to deal with a specific problem you encounter in a text?

Gunilla Anderman: People now know how to write if they want to be translated into English. There are certain ingredients that must be there. If you look around and see which works become bestsellers, you can see exactly what these ingredients are.

Said Faiq (Salford University): I agree with Paul that there are a number of general terms which are not solely part of one particular discipline but are shared by several disciplines. And certainly 'norms' is one of these terms. Regarding the acceptability of some texts and works, I think that 'great works' do tend to push translators or other people working on them to carve up a separate set of norms. You have the mainstream norms at work, but 'sensitive texts' tend to force their users to implement the mainstream norms in a different way.

Peter Newmark: I do not think that there are separate norms for the translation of 'great works'. If you mean by 'great works' serious and dramatic works, I would say that what you need is a closer method of translation, one where one would put in a minimum of new ideas and, because it is a great work, try to reproduce the ideas as much as possible. This might be a criterion of a good translation of a 'great work'.

Said Faiq: Let me add something else: I believe norms in general do not die. They just get recloned from generation to generation, or from one practice to another. They do not change, they are just revamped. In the past, norms used to live longer because there were borders, difficulties in travel and no communication. Nowadays, even with a vast development in technology, norms still suffer from power relationships and from censorship within communities. A related question to this is: who controls the norms? I think we should also look at the culture of norms and the norms used in the translation of cultures in general.

Gideon Toury: You have formulated some important questions. Where do norms come from? Do they develop within a group, or are norms imported? Has anything changed in this respect with the world becoming a 'global village'? The general answer would be 'yes', but this is not enough. We would like to see what changes have occurred, and how, and what power relationships have brought them about. You claim that norms do not change, they just get revamped. I would say that even if a norm assumedly stays the same, it is no longer the same norm because the constellation has changed. When a norm moves from a central position to the periphery, it is not the same norm any more. We have to look at the mechanisms of operation, not just at the fact that a certain norm is still there somewhere. We have to look at the relationships between the norms, at their hierarchical ordering, for example.

Norms and Translator Training

Peter Bush: I would like to ask how you relate the issue of norms to the training of translators? I think norms may be an important issue for the profession, both analytically, and also in an immediate sense for the training of translators.

Gideon Toury: We all train translators within the framework of normative models, and we all make decisions as to what the norms are going to be which we abide by, and which we want our students to abide by. The question is only, how dogmatic we are about it, whether only our own norms count or whether we would accept or reject a student's translation for which s/he used another set of norms. I think that many teachers would not accept it, although there are also teachers who are open to other approaches. Believe it or not, but in my own teaching and tutoring of teachers of translation, I am rather reactionist. I think that they should learn the tradition first, and improvise later. This is a conscious decision of mine, and I know it is not related to the outcome of my research. But I justify my approach because teaching and doing scholarly research are two different occupations.

Peter Bush: You are very good at compartmentalising. One of the difficulties I have as a teacher of translation, is that students are norm-conditioned, and in order to train them I have to say that they do not have to translate in one particular way. I have to build up their confidence so that they can translate challenging texts in the way that they wish to, and they find that very difficult. For example, if you give them a text by Dante, they don't want to translate it in an exciting way but rather in a very conformist way because it is a canonical text. I train students to become literary translators, and they have to translate texts which are written in the source culture deliberately against conventions. I have to make them aware of this. For example, the students on our MA course had an initial module, 'An introduction to academic discourse', in which they were told how to write academic discourse. But then I had to say to the translation students that this is not what literary translation is about. Academic discourse has to be written as academic discourse, but in order to become literary translators they also have to become writers. And in order to become writers they have to be able to work against that kind of academic discourse that has been the pinnacle of their university training.

Kirsten Malmkjær (University of Cambridge): Until five minutes ago, I did not think that norms were normative. I thought norms were more like Gricean maxims, and not like rules. I saw them as something that you discover after the event, as Gunilla said. This would seem to fit much better with your approach to teaching.

Gideon Toury: I think that everyone should be free to translate as they wish, and teachers should be given the freedom to teach within various approaches, but they should also know what their responsibilities are. This is an ethical issue, but not the solution to the ethical problem. The solution would need to come from each one of us. There are reasons why I decided to be much more conformist in my training, much more conformist than when I translate myself, because I know what the risks are. We have to think of the social role of norms. If you translate in an individual, non-conformist way, because that is what you were trained to do, you may not find a publisher, for example.

Peter Bush: I think you are missing my point. Students who come to postgraduate courses for literary translation do not come to that course as writers. They come from modern language courses where they were trained to become experts in whatever language they are going to translate from. They have to develop as writers. All I'm talking about is writing. I am not anarchic and saying 'do what you want', I am saying that you have to do research and study texts and you have to do all kinds of things. But the central part of what you do is that you have to be able to develop your own writing style. And to do that is very difficult in university contexts, and also in the context of a lot of discussion within translation studies which omits talking about this.

Gideon Toury: My experience is that most literary translators that I have studied so far do not act this way, even if they were very good writers themselves. In my experience, most of what has been called 'great literature' has not been translated in a non-conventional, or more advanced way. Most of Shakespeare's texts were translated into Hebrew by active poets and dramatists, i.e. by professional writers. But their translation of Shakespeare was done according to outdated norms. The texts look a lot older than their normal translations, let alone their original writings.

Peter Bush: I understand what you are saying, that there are writers who translate, and therefore they translate poetically. I am talking about the many people who are not recognised as public figures and as creative writers.

Theo Hermans: It seems to me that what you were saying about having to un-train novice translators lends itself to the question of norms. If we bear in mind the relativity of norms, the fact that they apply in certain circumstances to certain groups and not to others, then this point of view is quite liberating. You can tell students that if you do literary translation, then different norms apply than, for example, when you translate for the EU. And even within literature, there are differences between translating a novel or for the theatre. It is precisely because you can stress the relativity and changeability of norms that you can make them useful as a didactic tool.

Norms, Maxims and Conventions in Translation Studies and Pragmatics

Kirsten Malmkjær: I do not think that norms are something you follow in the same way that you follow rules. I do not think that norms are known, or if they are known, they are known subliminally. Gideon, you talk about a system of terminology which you have in order to guide your research. It would be helpful to not let the term norm have too wide a scope. I think it clouds the issue, because some people talk about norms as if they were prescriptive, whereas you use the term descriptively, in the sense that you have a text and on the basis of this you try to reconstruct the norms that guided its production.

Gideon Toury: Yes, but they are not too far removed from each other. What you assume you will find are norms that did have a prescriptive power.

Kirsten Malmkjær: But not in the sense that people have them fixed in their heads, so that you could tell your students 'this is the norm for translation in that country at that time'. If you look back at the hundreds of years tradition of Shakespeare translation you can see that at various points perhaps translators appear to have been guided by certain norms. I mentioned Grice because Grice and his maxims are often misunderstood in exactly the same way, so people refer to Grice and say look, there is a violation of his rules. But the maxims are not rules, and I think it's similar with your norms. They are not rules, but they are more like maxims. If there is an application to teaching, it is because you can show students the kinds of guidelines which people appear to have been guided by in the past.

Gideon Toury: This is what you can do in that part of a training programme where you look at translations that were done in the past and discuss the outcome. Once you come to workshops in practical translation you cannot start a discussion of historical issues.

Paul Chilton: I agree with Kirsten that it would be interesting to look at the Gricean maxims, or norms. In fact, there is the question as to whether the maxims are norms or whether they are the product of some kind of rational coordination and communication. Gideon, why do you choose to look at what you are interested in, in terms of norms, rather than approaching it through pragmatics and the Gricean maxims? Since translation is a form of linguistic behaviour, it would seem to find a natural home in pragmatics, and that it can be explained through the concepts for understanding communication that already exist there.

Gideon Toury: I myself have not worked with these maxims. I know that people have tried to apply them, and I have seen some attempt to apply them in manuscripts that were sent to our periodical *Target*. But all the applications that I have seen were bad, that is they were methodologically bad, not because of the results. This does not mean that it has anything to do with the notion of maxims as such, but the attempted applications have not contributed anything of significance.

Kirsten Malmkjær: I myself would hesitate to simply adopt translation studies under pragmatics. You could equally argue for placing translation under sociology, for example. But if you do this you lose sight of what is special to translation.

Christina Schäffner: I absolutely agree. It is just recently that translation studies has been gaining recognition as an academic discipline in its own right. Previously, and still today, it has been seen as a sub-discipline of applied linguistics, or of literary studies. It does build on insights, methods, and concepts from other disciplines, that's why the term 'interdiscipline' has been introduced, but there are so many aspects that are unique to translation that cannot be captured sufficiently by other disciplines.

Said Faiq: Translation studies can gain insights from text linguistics, discourse analysis, pragmatics, and so on. Translation is a meeting point of all these disciplines. There are a number of studies that provide frameworks that are not just applicable to translation, but to communication in general. But there is not yet any water-tight model of communication as such.

Theo Hermans: If we take a step back in time and think about the concept of translation as purely linguistic transfer, which dominated the debate 30 or 40 year ago, we have come a long way in appreciating the complexity of translation. Norms, for that reason also, are a very useful instrument. But it does raise the question of how to define norms. In contrast to Gideon, I have altered the notion and brought in the concept of convention. There is a definition of convention by David Lewis which is a useful way to start and then to build on and link it to norms. Apart from having a formal definition on which we can agree, the notion of convention has also been applied very widely in social sciences and also the arts. Lewis' definition has to do with regularities in behaviour, expectations, reciprocal expectations, and the anticipation of expectations. The difference between norm and convention is precisely that conventions are purely probabilistic expectations, there are no sanctions, whereas norms have a binding character. If you approach the issue in this way, you would probably get a better grip on the concept of norms, or at least agree on what you may mean by applying norms prescriptively or descriptively.

Gideon Toury: You are presenting conventions and norms as two parallel things, the only difference between them being the absence or presence of sanctions. I think that they belong to two different levels of observation. If conventions are to be realised, or if somebody needs to get trained and has to know what the conventions are, there is simply a need for norms as a link, as a way of transition into what the conventions are. Of course the conventions do not carry sanctions because they are not norms, but they are also somewhere else, metaphorically speaking. At present, I am not convinced that this distinction is helpful, but should the notion of convention help me work better, I would accept it.

Christina Schäffner: There is also the possibility of change and transition between the two concepts. Lewis himself said that norms can become conventions and conventions can become norms.

Theo Hermans: Yes, conventions can fall victim to their own success. In many cases it may be your decisions to label a particular regularity a convention or a weak norm. There is no clear borderline.

Reconstructing Norms

Jean-Pierre Mailhac (Salford University): I am interested in the methodology of norm reconstruction, in the descriptive sense. In your position paper you say that very often regularities seem to manifest themselves in rather low percentages. If this is the case, then it is not at all clear how significant they are. One would expect the task of extracting norms from the observed regularities to be carried out on a very substantial corpus, or several corpora, but in any case a substantial mass of data so that they are statistically meaningful. In this way you can also avoid any pitfalls that may be there, such as subjective emotions brought into norms, perhaps hidden agendas and so on. How do you go about reconstructing norms? Do you use large corpora, which we all know are extremely difficult to manipulate, even with computers? If not, what are the safeguards against the obvious pitfalls, and particularly if you are dealing with literary translation which is extremely fluid and complex. So how does one deal with these quantitative aspects of the analysis?

Gideon Toury: It is one thing to say what should be done in principle, but it is a completely different thing to say what is feasible within today's possibilities. In principle we can say the more, the better. There are, of course, limitations on the quantities of texts or phenomena which can be processed even with the aid of computers. I have mainly been working on translations into Hebrew, texts which are not easy to process mechanically, because the morphology is so complex. We are always working with samples, but even the problem of sampling is great, because the field in which we are working keeps changing and the quantities are enormous. There are two things I have been struggling with and for which I don't have any solution: the size of a sample on the one hand and the representativeness of a sample on the other hand. In my own practice I study lower-level phenomena, but in doing that I increase the percentages.

Peter Newmark: In all your talking about norms, I am missing the examples. See if you accept one simple norm, and I think a very common one, namely the common translation of the French preposition 'grâce à' automatically as 'thanks to'. That appears to me to be a simple example which you may quarrel with.

Gideon Toury: When you find that in 100 per cent of the cases in your sample 'grâce à' has been translated by 'thanks to' than you have findings with respect to a very minor phenomenon, although I hesitate to say that this is a realisation of a norm.

Peter Newmark: But will you give me a norm then?

Gideon Toury: Elevation of style, unification of style. It is this level that I'm striving for. But as I said, I have done some studies on lower level phenomena. As a matter of fact, I studied the use of discourse connectors in translations into Hebrew in comparison with original Hebrew texts, although this was done in the 1970s, and without the help of computers. It was obvious that in translations the distribution of these markers was much denser than in any original writing. The next question was, why was this the case? Finally, after some more studies, I found out that many of them were simply translated literally, that is not as pragmatic markers but as semantic units. Now you may ask me what the norm is, but I do not know how to formulate it because I suspect that it goes way beyond the pragmatic structures. On the other hand, when you take the corpus and you break it up, for example into decades, and if then you find that the patterns change, then you will find interesting things. You still do not know how to formulate the norm itself, but then you know what happened to this anonymous norm, or what happened in the translational behaviour over time with regard to this particular phenomenon.

Jean-Pierre Mailhac: Let me link on from the quantitative to the qualitative dimension in the reconstruction of the data. You start from a sociological point of view which implies that groups or social constituencies must be linked to the textual data. If you do studies on, for example, insurance texts, you have a type of text which is very clearly defined and you also have a very clearly defined social constituency of people that use these texts. But if you are dealing with literary texts, things tend to be much more complex. The interesting example given by Paul Chilton showed that there were different norms involved and different constituencies linked to each norm. With literary texts, how do you make the link between the textual data and the social constituencies?

Gideon Toury: First of all, I do not think that literature is all that different from other kinds of texts. I myself have mainly translated literature, and I think that very often the translation of other text types involves a lot more than translating literature does. The whole point is that we as researchers approach the translations, and not the problems in the original. Once you approach the translations, it is much easier to group them. For example, for my dissertation, written in Hebrew in 1976, I did a preliminary study in which I gave profiles of three leading publishing houses at that time, and I could prove a one-to-one correlation between the behaviour of the translator as observed in the translated text, and the publisher who issued it. The difficult part was knowing what the translator actually did. Maybe some formulations were not done by the translator, but were the result of an editing process to make the text fit into the framework of this publishing house. This is again a problem where subjectivity is circumstantial, but there is no other way of doing it, unless you have access to the archives of the publishing houses, but in my case none of them had any archives for that period. All you can do then is to start from the translations and go backwards, not knowing how many hands were involved in the production of the text, nor how many processes. What I had to do was to look at drafts, edited versions, proofs etc., thus breaking it all down into layers. I have been working on one of the translations into Hebrew of one of the versions of *Don Quixote*, translated into Hebrew not from Spanish but from German. This translation was always praised by critics for its strictly biblical style. In Hebrew this means something very precise. But I found out in the drafts that the translator had enormous difficulties with this. It became clear that the norm he was aiming at was writing in biblical Hebrew, but he had difficulties achieving it. So the first draft is something completely different, and in the editing processes he changed his attitude, and he found his voice.

Margaret Rogers (University of Surrey): I would like to link these points of authority and norms to the classroom situation. In your discussion paper, you have a remark that when someone who is beginning to learn to translate does something which is innovative it would usually be recorded as 'erroneous'. This is analogous to what happens with non-native speakers with regard to native speakers in language learning. When in an essay the non-native speaker comes up with a collocation which is not typically used, it is usually marked as wrong. The question is then: who has the authority to introduce a change? Authority, in my opinion, is a movable feast, and this comes back to the question of community we have had earlier. If you take the example of 'Euro-speak', native speakers of British English react sometimes highly negatively to the innovations which are coming through from the European Community, where documents are written in English by non-native speakers or translated into English and influenced by the source language. In this process, obviously changes occur, and as a result sometimes very useful new concepts are introduced. But who is the authority here? Certainly not the native speaker of English but the institutions of the European Community. My point is that if we continually redefine the community from which the authority derives, doesn't it become too powerful a concept?

Gideon Toury: The community changes all the time, and what constitutes a community varies in different societies and different periods of time. It is part of the research project to find out what the source of power is. I cannot assume *a priori* that I know what a source of power would be in a particular case because there is no such thing as an unchanging source of power. Power comes from different sources at different times, and there is also a struggle for domination. The first study I ever did as a student was into deviant uses of collocations in Hebrew. I found cases in which the very same modifications were highly praised because they came from the pen of an acknowledged journalist or writer, and the same things in pupils' essays were marked wrong. Whether changes that were introduced by a translator are accepted or not is also related to the relative power, credibility, status of translator, which, however, is very often not particularly high.

Translation and Normativity

Theo Hermans
University College London, Gower Street, London WC1E 6BT, UK

The article has two main aims: to illustrate the productive potential of the norms concept as an analytical tool in studying translations, and to explore the implications of the concept for the way we speak about translation. Part one takes up an historical case (Adrianus de Buck translating Boethius in 1653) and uses the concept of norms to inquire into the translator's choices. It is suggested that sociological concepts deployed by Bourdieu and Luhmann may offer useful ways forward in applying norm concepts as tools to study translation. Part two begins by positing a connection between norms and values. If translation is norm-governed it cannot be value-free. Three points are discussed following from this. First, its lack of transparency is what makes translation significant as a cultural and historical phenomenon. Second, the notion of equivalence can only be an ideological construct. Its presence in the historical discourse on translation is worth investigating, for it reveals key aspects of the conceptual self-positioning of translation. Finally, if our speaking about translation is itself a form of translating, then the implication must be that our translations of translation cannot be value-free either.

Introduction

So much has been written in the last 20 years about norms and their relevance to translation that it is reasonable to assume at least a certain familiarity with the concept of norms as such (cf. Baker, 1998 for a concise statement and references). Allow me therefore to preface my remarks with no more than a brief reminder, in the form of a quotation from Thomas Merton's 1942 essay, 'The Normative Structure of Science'. It is a very traditional statement in more ways than one, but Merton's definition of 'the ethos of science' in terms of values and norms can readily be translated from the world of the sciences into that of translation:

> The ethos of science is that affectively toned complex of values and norms which is held to be binding on the man of science. The norms are expressed in the form of prescriptions, proscriptions, preferences, and permissions. They are legitimized in terms of institutional values. These imperatives, transmitted by precept and example and reenforced by sanctions, are in varying degrees internalized by the scientist, thus fashioning his scientific conscience or, if one prefers the latter-day phrase, his super-ego. Although the ethos of science has not been codified, it can be inferred from the moral consensus of scientists as expressed in use and wont, in countless writings on the scientific spirit and in moral indignation directed toward contraventions of the ethos. (Merton, 1973: 268–69)

With respect to translation, the expression of norms in the form of prescriptions, proscriptions, preferences and permissions, their legitimation in terms of institutional values, their transmission through precept and example, their reinforcement by means of sanctions, and their overall regulative function, have all been extensively debated and documented, both in general terms and with reference to a number of individual cases. There is not much point in going over this familiar ground (cf. Hermans, 1996b). Rather than rehearse the basic ideas and review the work done so far, I should therefore like to do two things. First, I want to suggest the productive potential of the norms concept as an analytical tool in the historical study of translation, highlighting one or two aspects that have perhaps not received the attention they deserve. After this methodological section I will go on to consider some theoretical and meta-theoretical implications of the norms concept and their relevance to the way we think and speak about translation.

Let me start by looking at one historical example, to see what illumination, if any, there is to be had from a norms-based approach to it. My aim is to suggest that even when we are dealing with a single translation, an approach via the concept of norms can be fruitful in generating questions about and directing attention to certain aspects of the case. My focus will be on the translator's choices against a background of a limited range of practically available alternatives, and on the possible reasons why a particular option was selected from among that range. The privileging of selectivity has two distinct advantages. On the one hand, the choices which the translator makes simultaneously highlight the exclusions, the paths that were open but that were *not* chosen. On the other, the approach sheds light on the interplay between the translator's responses to existing expectations, constraints and pressures, and his or her intentional, goal-directed action or agency.

De Buck's Boethius

The case I want to present is of no great historical moment at all. Indeed it suits the purposes of illustration precisely because it is so utterly unremarkable, with the exception perhaps of one or two intriguing features that I intend to milk for all they are worth.

It concerns a seventeenth-century Flemish Catholic priest, one Adrianus de Buck, an obscure and now forgotten figure. Biographical details are almost entirely lacking. We know of only two publications by him: a book of prayers, and his translation, in 1653, of Boethius' *Consolation of Philosophy*, rendered from Latin into Dutch. The translation — of which there are only two known extant copies — appeared in Bruges, i.e. in the Southern Netherlands then still under Catholic Spanish rule. Around the mid-sixteenth century the whole of the Low Countries had been ruled by the Spanish Habsburgs. In the 1560s an armed rebellion had broken out which, at one point, engulfed the entire area. The southern part (roughly, contemporary Belgium) eventually returned to the Catholic fold and to Spanish rule. The Calvinist-dominated Northern Netherlands had emerged as a *de facto* independent republic in the 1590s. In the course of the first half of the seventeenth century, the north became astonishingly prosperous and powerful, witnessing the explosion of creative talent that produced the likes of Rembrandt and Vermeer. Spain formally recognised the Dutch Republic as a sovereign state in 1648.

De Buck's translation of Boethius contains a dedication to a number of local dignitaries, a number of other liminary texts including the usual approbations and laudatory poems, and the main text in prose and verse. In his dedication (reprinted in Hermans, 1996a: 121–3) the translator leaves us in no doubt that he is green with envy at the miracle of Dutch culture in the Northern Netherlands, not least because, he says, they have appropriated the learning of every other language in the world, including Greek, Hebrew, Turkish and Arabic. In other words, de Buck was acutely aware of living in what, by comparison with the thriving republic in the North, was rapidly becoming a cultural backwater. Politically, too, the area was weak and vulnerable. The military threat, however, came not from the north but from the south, from France. Indeed the Southern Netherlands were experiencing the effects of France's expansionism. The small town of Veurne, where de Buck was living, is near the French border. It had been overrun a few years earlier by the armies of Louis XIV and Cardinal Mazarin, and was still occupied. Negotiations for a peaceful settlement had started but were not getting anywhere.

And so de Buck has now translated Boethius. He has done so, he tells us in the dedication, for several reasons: partly to offer consolation to his compatriots who have suffered at the hands of the French, partly because he reckons that the Protestant heretics in the North have left Boethius untranslated on account of the references to free will and to purgatory in the *Consolation*, and partly also because he wants to prove that, as he puts it, 'the sun also shines on our West-Flemish land and there is fire in our souls too' (... *dat oock het West-Vlaender-landt van de Sonne beschenen wordt, ende dat'er oock vlamme woont in onse zielen*). I will try to interpret these statements below. The translation itself follows the prose and verse in Boethius' Latin with corresponding prose and verse. The verse translations exhibit one curious feature: de Buck has rendered several of the poems in Boethius not once but twice, in two different metres.

Since a norms-based approach to translation starts from the assumption that the translation process involves decision-making on the part of the translator, it will focus on the question of what choices are made in relation to available alternatives, and what it is that steers translators towards one preferred option rather than another. I take it for granted that when we speak of norms we include the entire range from strict rules down to conventions (or 'quasi-norms', as Poltermann, 1992: 17 calls them), the latter without a binding character backed up by sanctions (for a formal definition of 'convention', see Lewis, 1969). In addition, I want to think of norms not only as regularities in behaviour and a certain degree of pressure exercised on the individual to prefer one option rather than another, but also as sets of expectations about preferred options, and as the anticipation of such expectations, i.e. as the expectation of expectations. Finally, I like to think that the teleological aspect of translator behaviour comes into its own as translators consciously or unconsciously negotiate their way through and around existing norm complexes with a view to securing some form of benefit, whether personal or collective, material or symbolic.

In discussing de Buck's Boethius, I will look first at the selection of the source text, and then at de Buck's mode of translating. In this latter respect I will consider both de Buck's own comments on how he has translated some parts of his source text and at his actual practice. My argument will be, roughly, that de Buck is catering for three overlapping but not necessarily identical constituencies. He is writing, firstly, for his compatriots as political subjects, as fellow sufferers at the hands of the French, emphasising the consolation to be had from reading Boethius. Secondly, he addresses them as co-religionists and self-conscious

Catholics, dramatically claiming Boethius for the Counter-Reformation. Thirdly, he speaks to them as cultural agents, a culturally aware audience who may well be concerned, as he is, about the cultural dominance of the Northern Netherlands. Accordingly, in de Buck's Boethius we can trace different norms, political, religious and cultural, with different degrees of force, informing his decisions. At the same time we can read the way in which the translator negotiates the options in front of him as a strategy, a matter of goal-oriented calculation in order to achieve particular aims.

We can view de Buck's choice of Boethius as a source text in relation to the primary function of the translation. As de Buck explains in his preface, he wants to render a service to his compatriots as political subjects and fellow citizens. Although he does not tell us in so many words, we can safely interpret de Buck's decision to offer a translation in the first place, and not to write something of his own invention, against the background of the commonly held Renaissance view that to transmit the tried and tested sayings of some valued authority is often preferable to producing your own laborious and probably inept invention. For someone like de Buck, a provincial priest with (as far as I can tell) no long-term ambition to make his mark as a writer, the translating option must have seemed a fairly obvious choice.

Why Boethius? Just as Boethius drew comfort from philosophical speculation at a time when he was in prison awaiting execution, so the hard-pressed citizens of Flanders will derive consolation from reading Boethius in their hour of need. That is what makes Boethius an apt choice for de Buck, in preference to an unspecified number of alternative possibilities. Just how many alternatives were realistically available to de Buck is obviously impossible to ascertain. The list will almost certainly have included works such as Justus Lipsius' *De constantia* of 1584. Lipsius was a Catholic writer and enjoyed international fame as a Humanist at Louvain University, barely 50 miles from de Buck's town of Veurne. The *De constantia*, a dialogue in the Stoic tradition, had been written, like Boethius's *Consolation*, to find equanimity amid a sea of troubles and proved an immediate European bestseller. However, the book was readily accessible to de Buck's compatriots in a popular Dutch translation, with editions in 1584, 1621 and 1640 (Hoven, 1997). In other words, highlighting obvious but excluded alternatives allows us to appreciate the significance of de Buck's selection, as we can see him making his own choice optimally relevant in view of what is already available in terms of suitable source texts. In providing solace and a morale-booster his translation constitutes an answer to a perceived problem. To emphasise the point his preface develops several apposite metaphors related to wounds and healing, and to loss of material goods as being outweighed by the retention of spiritual values.

Two other aspects of de Buck's choice of Boethius gain relief when we pick up his comments on the cultural and translational practices in the Northern Netherlands. De Buck notes that Boethius is not selected for translation there, and that this is for religious reasons: the references to free will are unacceptable to Calvinist doctrine.[1] His awareness of this ideological aspect makes his own choice deliberate, but also oppositional, differential, polemical. His Boethius contributes to the differentiation of the Southern translational tradition *vis-à-vis* the Northern one, and this will have further ideological, political and religious repercussions as regards expectations about translated as well as other texts. Boethius, in this particular translation, emphatically Catholic and with some translational peculiarities like the 'double' rendering of some of the poems, is now becoming part of the Southern cultural landscape. Since the number of practically available options for placing Boethius in a religious and philosophical context is limited (Boethius as a universal Christian? As a moral philosopher? As a Neo-Platonist? As a Protestant thinker despite appearances?), de Buck's pointed appropriation of him as Catholic also brings out these exclusions. Moreover, the ease with which Boethius could be claimed as a Catholic writer may well have made him preferable as a source to, say, Seneca or another Stoic.

In addition to identifying religion as a significant point of difference between a Protestant North and a Catholic South, de Buck's choice of Boethius also contributes to the ongoing refashioning of the Southern cultural tradition as a whole. It constitutes one small move in the deployment of translation, as of other cultural resources, in support of the militant Counter-Reformation. The strict criteria for text production prevalent in the political and religious spheres in the Spanish Netherlands are imposed on — or, from de Buck's point of view, eagerly imported into — the cultural and translational domain, in this case in the form of criteria for source text selection. Boethius is emphatically presented as a Catholic writer. De Buck's selection is clearly governed by, and in turn strengthens already strong normative constraints. The selection is both structured and structuring. The constraints themselves are ideological in nature and resemble those prevalent in Spain and the rest of Catholic Europe at the time, rather than those of the more tolerant Dutch Republic. And as de Buck allies himself with Counter-Reformation Europe, he simultaneously opposes the Protestant North.

If a translation offers a verbal representation of an anterior text across a semiotic boundary, and typically a representation such that it can serve as a full-scale re-enactment of its source across an intelligibility barrier, then every translation constitutes a selection of a particular mode of representation from among a wider range of available, permissible modes. The set of permissible modes — the ensemble we also refer to as the 'constitutive' norms and conventions of translation — circumscribes the concept of translation in the world of which de Buck is a part. The selection which he makes will determine the words on the page, the translation's specific verbal orchestration or 'style'. As was the case with source text selection, the choice of a particular style or representational mode highlights the exclusions going with it, and thus points up the existence of alternative possibilities, of paths not chosen, as well as of certain stylistic and representational allegiances, similar choices made by other writers and translators. In de Buck's Boethius some of these allegiances and exclusions are made explicit. They are thematised, or dramatised, both in the translator's preface and in the unusual decision to render some of the Latin poems twice, in two different forms.

In his preface de Buck informs us that he has translated the title of Boethius' book 'in an explanatory manner' (*tot breeder verklaringh*). Indeed, what in Latin reads as a book 'on the consolation of philosophy' (*De consolatione philosophiae liber*) has in Dutch been expanded into a 'comforting medicine shop of moral wisdom' (*Troost-Medecijne-wynckel der zedighe wysheyt*). The expansive rendering stresses the aspect of healing and the practical usefulness of moral philosophy. For de Buck this more paraphrastic mode is clearly a legitimate form of translating, which suggests that the concept of 'translation' he is operating with is already internally differentiated, marked by various sets of 'regulatory' (as opposed to 'constitutive') norms and conventions. Apart from the standard mode of translating, which apparently does not require comment, there is also this other mode. The paraphrastic rendering of the title would here seem to be a matter of convention only, a personal preference within an area of relatively free variation. Since he wants to emphasise the soothing effect that comes from practical moral philosophy, he avails himself of an existing, permissible mode of translation to achieve that goal.

Equally paraphrastical (*een luttel wijdt-loopigh*, 'somewhat long-drawn-out'), de Buck tells us, are the renderings of some of the verses which he confesses he sometimes found very hard to grasp in the Latin even after consulting learned commentaries, on account of the abstruse mixture of Aristotelian and Platonic ideas which they contain. The reason for the paraphrastic mode in this instance appears to lie in the elucidation of conceptual obscurity.

The fact, however, that in both these cases he feels the need explicitly to justify his recourse to a paraphrastic mode with reference to specific places and specific reasons suggests that, although it is a legitimate form of translating and hence one that meets existing expectations about what constitutes translation, i.e. one that stays within the perimeter policed by the constitutive norms and conventions of translation, de Buck recognises it as more marginal than the 'standard' mode of translating. This is presumably because paraphrase, requiring the translator to speak more overtly in his or her own name, tends to forms such as glossing, commentary, or imitation. These forms are all adjacent to, may occasionally overlap with but are definitely not coterminous with the prevailing concept of translation. In other words, through de Buck's comments the boundaries of translation as he, and presumably a number of his contemporaries understand them, come clearly into view as well.

Then there are the 'double' translations, in two different metres, of some of the poems. This procedure is, without a doubt, unusual and unexpected. It is not entirely unknown at the time, but normally found in personal albums or commonplace books, and associated with shorter, highly crafted literary forms such as epigrams. The option to translate verse into verse is undoubtedly dictated by a norm, but since different verse forms are available to the translator (indeed Boethius employs different metres) the choice for a particular form appears to be a question of convention. De Buck does not tell us why he chose to translate some poems twice. It may be that we have to see his decision in light of his statements about paraphrastic translation. But then the question arises: why two *verse* forms? If conceptual elucidation by means of loose paraphrase was the aim, prose would have been a more obvious and equally available choice. To my mind — and this is very much a matter of speculation — the 'double' renderings do not primarily serve the translation's function as representation. Rather, they do two things. Firstly, they dramatise the fact that there *are* alternative possibilities, demonstrating that choice in this instance is merely a matter of convention; secondly, and more importantly, they serve as displays of virtuosity to underscore a claim to professional equality *vis-à-vis* the translators in the North.

As for the first point, in providing an emphatic comment on free choice within the bounds of permissible translational modes, the dual renderings remind the reader that the translation's basic function, that of providing a serviceable representation of an otherwise inaccessible source text, allows in practice for more than one stylistic option, at least as far as the verse is concerned. Both poetic forms which de Buck is offering are presented as valid; both remain metrical, though. Since there is no suggestion that the two options which he has chosen exhaust the range of valid modes, his practice signals a degree of tolerance in the choice of poetic form to render poetic form. Subsequent translators may want to act on de Buck's precedent and take up either or both models that he has supplied. To the extent that future reader expectations are affected by de Buck's example, however, they will be cognitive rather than normative expectations, within a normatively circumscribed range of acceptable verse forms.

But de Buck's 'double' translation also supports a conspicuous bid for recognition and legitimacy by a Southern translator *vis-à-vis* what he evidently perceives as the more successful tradition in the North. By demonstrating virtuosity in verse translation the practitioner in the weaker system can claim professional equality with translators in the dominant system, while still distancing himself in religious and therefore in ideological terms. In this respect too, de Buck may well be exploiting the opportunity offered by the absence of a strong normative constraint governing the choice of a particular verse form in verse translation.

In passing, and on a very different level, let me also note that the 'double' translation introduces a discursive complication into the text. From a standard communicative point of view the repetition is redundant; even if the reader finds it useful as a help to understanding complex theological and philosophical ideas, its occurrence clearly undermines the illusion that we are reading Boethius and registering only a single voice as we do so. The translator's presence in the text is unmistakable. In thus drawing attention to the translator's presence as a discursive subject, the Dutch text reveals its hybrid, plurivocal nature.

As far as the prose passages are concerned, here de Buck evidently had other priorities: providing solace, and vindicating Boethius as a Catholic author. That is why his vocabulary here borrows directly from the terminological and discursive resources of Catholic theology and liturgy. In so doing de Buck also helps to consolidate the hegemony of Catholic discourse in the vernaculars of Counter-Reformation Europe. But it is worth bearing in mind that what is alliance in one direction, that of Catholic, southern Europe, is self-assertion through deliberate competition and emphatic differentiation in another, i.e. that of the Protestant Dutch Republic.

In de Buck's case, of course, the alliance with the values of the Counter-Reformation Church is unsurprising. He was a Catholic priest. Lay translators in the Spanish Netherlands, however, in marked contrast with those in the more tolerant and decentralised North, would not have had appreciably more room for manoeuvre. In their case the ideological pressure might be less enthusiastically internalised and hence their behaviour more immediately inspired by the wish to avoid sanctions and censorship. The results would have been the same.

Translation, Norms and Values

There is more in de Buck's Boethius that merits attention, but let us leave the discussion of this particular translation and briefly review the gain that may be derived from a case like this. Several things could be singled out.

The first point is an obvious one. The example can serve to suggest the heuristic relevance of proceeding with a norms concept as a guiding tool. This does not mean using norms as causal explanations. It does mean exploring the whole range from conventions to norms to decrees, in different, intersecting spheres and on different, interconnected levels, to see how they bear on the decisions involved in the translation process. It also means weighing external pressures, acquired habits and routinely applied skills against the individual's presumed goal-oriented design in particular circumstances. Determining what factor or aspect is most relevant in individual instances is likely to remain a matter of interpretation and speculation. It is, as always, the observer who constructs the case before him or her, rendering data relevant by deploying them as evidence.

Secondly, focusing on norms not primarily as regularities in behaviour extracted from large corpora but as a matter of prevailing normative as well as cognitive expectations, and the selective aspect of the individual translator's choice for a particular option in the context of a limited range of realistically available alternatives, allows for the use of the concepts of norms and conventions as a way of asking questions not only about what is there on the page but also about what might have been there but, for one reason or another, is not. Trying to figure out what those reasons might be can prove illuminating. Assessing the exclusions makes us appreciate the significance of the inclusions.

But it is time to open up the perspective. It seems to me that there are currently several broader theoretical frameworks that could give added resonance to the norms concept as it has been used hitherto in the study of translation. Some of these already left echoes in my discussion of de Buck's Boethius. For example, my emphasis on de Buck's choices as meaningful selections in a differential context, i.e. as acquiring meaning through their selectivity and thus against the background of the more or less likely alternatives that were excluded, is indebted to the social systems theory of Niklas Luhmann, as is the stress on norms reinterpreted in terms of expectations (Luhmann, 1984, 1986, 1990). For Luhmann, social systems consist of communications which connect over time; normative as well as cognitive expectations about communications form the structure of a social system. However, I do not want to elaborate here on Luhmann's complex and quite abstract systems theory, as this would lead us too far afield. Suffice it to say that Luhmann's voluminous writings on social systems have been applied to areas ranging from ecology and education to art history. I can see no reason why they could not be applied to the world of translation.[2]

The other name to be mentioned here is that of Pierre Bourdieu. For all the substantial differences between Luhmann and Bourdieu, both are sociologists who think primarily in relational terms, and both are alive to issues of language and culture. As far as translational norms are concerned, it is perfectly possible to view their acquisition by the individual translator in Bourdieu's terms as the inculcation of a durable, transposable disposition, i.e. a *habitus* which is both structured and structuring, forming a link between the individual and the social (Bourdieu, 1994, 1996). In the same way the translator's manoeuvering within and between norm complexes prevalent in a particular field lends itself to description in terms of Bourdieu's concept of social positions and position-takings, the accumulation of symbolic or other capital and the struggle for the monopoly of defining 'translation'.[3]

Within the broadly descriptive and historicising approach to translation, the elaboration of concepts derived from sociological theories like those of Luhmann or Bourdieu seems a promising and exciting prospect to me. The eminently 'social' notion of norms, assimilated into expectations or dispositions, offers an obvious point of departure. But there is also another dimension which the notion of translational norms opens up.

As we know, social conventions, norms and rules are intimately tied up with *values*. The content of a norm is a notion of what a particular community regards as correct or proper. The directive force of a norm is there to secure and maintain these notions as values. The assumption is roughly that norms serve as the active ingredient by means of which general values are transmuted into guidelines and prompters for concrete action. The dominant values, and hence the dominant norms, of communities tend to reflect the hierarchies of power in those communities.

If norms, understood in this sense, are relevant to acts of translation, then translation can never be value-free. The example of de Buck's Boethius will have made that abundantly clear. In claiming Boethius as a Catholic (and therefore emphatically not a Protestant or a universal Christian) writer, the translator shows his perception to be ideological, perspectival, slanted, overdetermined, manipulative. When de Buck then translates Boethius, the dislocation brought about is ideological as well as linguistic, temporal, geographical and communicative. And this is inevitable: we can only perceive and make sense of the world from our own point of view. Moreover, since translation invariably caters for other discourses, it has to reckon with the norms and values that prevail in the social domains sustained by those discourses. This means that the representations and re-enactments produced by translation cannot be transparent or ideologically neutral. Through the operation of norms they incorporate the values that gave rise to them in the first place.

On that basis I want to suggest three points. First, what makes translation interesting as a cultural phenomenon is precisely its lack of transparency, i.e. its opacity and complicity. Secondly, if translation always puts a slant on representation, then retaining the notion of equivalence in critical thinking about translation becomes problematical. And thirdly, if equivalence is discredited, what needs to be explained is why it has played and continues to play such a key part in the common perception and the self-presentation of translation.

Translation as an Index of Self-Reference

As for the first point, we know that translations appropriate, transform and relocate their source texts, adjusting them to new communicative situations and purposes. Just how much and what kind of attuning is prescribed, proscribed, preferred or permitted in practice, will depend on prevailing concepts of translation, including their normative aspects, and on who has the power to impose them.

The specific way in which a community construes translation therefore determines the way in which individual translations refer to their prototexts, the kind of image of the original which translations project. The 'anterior text' to which a translation refers is never simply the source text, even though that is the claim which translations commonly make. It is a particular image of it, as André Lefevere (1992) argued. And because the image is always slanted, coloured, pre-formed, never innocent, we can say that translation constructs or produces or, in Tejaswini Niranjana's words (1992: 81), 'invents' its original. A culture's value system together with the norm complexes which serve to hold it in its place, see to it that translation is governed by at least three normative levels: general cultural and ideological norms which may be held to apply throughout the larger part of a community; translational norms arising from general concepts of translatability and cross-lingual representation alive in that community; and the textual and other appropriateness norms which prevail in the particular client system for which individual translations cater.

If this is true, then the whole cognitive and normative apparatus which governs the selection, production and reception of translations, together with the way in which translation generally is circumscribed and regulated at a certain historical moment, presents us with a privileged index of cultural self-reference. In reflecting about itself, a cultural community defines its identity in terms of self and other, establishing the differential boundary in the process. Translation offers a window on cultural self-reference in that it involves not simply the importation of selected cultural goods from the outside world, or indeed their imposition on others, but at the same time, in the same breath as it were, their transformation on the basis of and into terms which are always loaded, never innocent. Translation is of interest precisely because it offers first-hand evidence of the prejudice of perception and of the pervasiveness of local concerns. If translations were neutral, transparent, unproblematical, they would be dull and uninformative, either in themselves or as documents of cultural history and the history of ideas. They would be about as interesting as xerox machines. But because they are opaque, complicitous and compromised, the history of translation supplies us with a highly charged, revealing series of cultural constructions of otherness, and therefore of self. Being non-transparent, translations perhaps tell us more about those who translate than about the source text underlying the translation. It is the bias built into the practice of translation, the uses made of translation and the ways in which translation is conceptualised, that gives insight into how cultures perceive and place themselves.

In this perspective it is relevant to note that the very notion of translatability already contains an assumption of the commensurability of languages and cultures. Resistance or indifference to translation, or the absence of translation where it was an option, or indeed the claim to untranslatability, are as informative as the pursuit of this or that particular type of translation. And it is useful to bear in mind that when translation occurs it is always a particular, circumscribed and often institutionally transmitted type of translation. Translators never 'just translate'. They translate in the context of certain conceptions of and expectations about translation, however much they may take them for granted or come to regard them as natural. Within this context translators make choices and take up positions because they have certain goals to reach, personal or collective interests to pursue, material and symbolic stakes to defend. That is where the concrete interplay of the personal and the collective takes place. As the norms concept constantly reminds us, translators, like those who use or commission translations, are social agents.

Equivalence and Difference

Let me go on to my second point, the issue of equivalence. One of the reasons why Gideon Toury's introduction of the norms concept into the study of translation has proved to be of such strategic importance was that it has directed attention away from the vexed notion of equivalence and focused instead on the factors governing the choices that determined the relation between source and target texts. In Toury's words: 'norms [...] determine the (type and extent of) equivalence manifested by actual translations' (1995: 61). Equivalence has thus effectively been sidelined, and demoted. In the traditional approach equivalence was posited as both the aim and precondition of translation: every translation was thought to strive to attain equivalence, and only those renderings which achieved equivalence of the required kind to a sufficient degree could be qualified as translations. In Toury's empirical approach it is reduced to a mere label designating the outcome of an operation which for one reason or another has been taken to constitute translation. Since Toury is keen — and rightly so — to cover 'the possibility of accounting for every kind of behaviour which may be culturally regarded as translational' he employs the term 'equivalence' to mean 'any relation which is found to have characterised translation under a specified set of circumstances' (1995: 61), or, more fully: equivalence is 'a *functional-relational* concept' standing for 'that set of relationships which will have been found to distinguish appropriate from inappropriate modes of translation performance for the culture in question' (1995: 86).

Having hollowed out the notion of equivalence to such an extent, Toury has decided nevertheless to hang on to it. Indeed he expresses 'a clear wish to retain the notion of equivalence', even though it has now been reduced to an 'historical' concept (1995: 61). And he repeats elsewhere that the study of individual translations will 'proceed from the assumption that equivalence does exist between an assumed translation and its assumed source', adding again that 'what remains to be uncovered is only the way this postulate was actually realized' (1995: 86).

Now, when we consider the primary role of norms and values in the perception and cross-lingual refashioning of source texts, it seems to me that retaining the notion of equivalence as the outcome of translation and then simply moving on, has unfortunate consequences. First stripping equivalence down to a mere label and then re-introducing it by the back door without further questioning the term's implications, blurs precisely the aspect of non-equivalence, of manipulation, dislocation and displacement which the norms concept did so much to push into the foreground. This blurring of non-equivalence is unfortunate for two reasons.

First, it is the aspect of non-equivalence which constantly reminds us that the whole process of cultural contact and transmission of which translation forms part is governed by norms and values, and by what lies behind them: power, hierarchy, non-equality. As postcolonial approaches to cultural history have shown again and again, relations between communities and cultures are never relations between equals. The refusal of some contemporary Irish poets to have their work translated into English, an obvious instance of the political significance of non-translation, occurs in a context in which languages like English and Irish are not on an equal footing. In the years following 1513 the so-called 'Requerimiento' which informed the American Indians of their place in the Spanish empire was read to them in Spanish only; any translations into local languages faced not just the linguistic and cultural displacement that translation brings with it, but at the same time their lack of legal validity. Around the turn of the nineteenth century the decrees issued by the revolutionary French regime in annexed territories like Belgium were in French only; while in the Flemish region translations into Dutch appeared alongside the French, only the French version possessed legal force. To speak of equivalence in such cases, with its suggestion of equal value, is like speaking of translation as exchange, or as bridge-building, suggesting fairness, friendship and two-way processes but obscuring translation's one-directionality and its complicity in relations of power. Even if semantic equivalence is granted, that aspect cannot undo the simultaneous non-equivalence in other, equally relevant respects which pertain to the status and role, and therefore the sense and significance, of translations.

The second point is more paradoxical. Just as Luhmann has observed that what needs to be explained is the improbability of communication, given the many good reasons why it is unlikely to succeed, so it seems to me that what needs to be explained as regards translation is *not* what kind and extent of equivalence is manifested by translations, but why, in the face of glaring linguistic, cultural and other differences, concepts of translation have nonetheless emerged in which equivalence can still be posited, even taken for granted and given prominence. By retaining equivalence in our critical vocabulary, even in a watered-down version, we sidestep that issue, we make it impossible even to ask the question. The norms concept however should serve as a reminder that it is difference, not sameness or transparency or equality, which is inscribed in the operations of translation. Starting from difference as a prime condition, we need to account for the occurrence and durability of the unlikely notion of equivalence. One way of doing this, I suggest, is to consider equivalence as part of the cultural construction of translation.

We tend to think of translation in terms of relayed communication. The translator acts as a relay station: enabler, conduit and transformer at the same time. On this side of the language barrier we feel we can place our trust in the translator's mediating role because we assume that the transformation leaves the source message essentially intact. Although we realise that the original and the translation are not quite identical, we trust the translator's competence, integrity and good faith, and hence assume that this integrity extends to the substitute message we are being offered: it must be a faithful reproduction, a reliable duplicate, a quality replica. The standard metaphors of translation incessantly rehearse these aspects in casting translation, on the one hand, as bridge building, ferrying or carrying across, transmission, transfer, 'trans-latio', 'meta-phor', and, on the other, as resemblance, likeness, mimesis. A translation may be a derived product, a mere copy and therefore secondary, second-hand and second-best, but as long as there is nothing to jolt us out of our willing suspension of disbelief we assume that to all intents and purposes the replica is virtually 'as good as' and therefore equivalent with the real thing.

To the extent that translations manage to produce, or to project, a sense of equivalence, a sense of transparency and trustworthiness which entitles them to function as full-scale representations and hence as reliable substitutes for their source texts, statements like 'I have read Dostoevsky' pass as legitimate shorthand for saying 'I have actually read a translation of Dostoevsky', with the implication 'and this is practically as good as reading the original'. But note: only to the extent that a 'sense' of equivalence, of equality in practical use value, has been produced (cf. Pym, 1995). And we tend to believe that this 'sense' of equivalence results from the reliability of the translation as reproduction, as resemblance, as transparency. A translation, we say, is most successful when its being a translation does not get in the way, does not distract, does not detract from our presumption of integrity. A translation most coincides with its original when it is most transparent, when it approximates pure resemblance.

This requires that the translator's labour leave no identifiable trace of its own, that it be negated or sublimated. The irony is, of course, that those traces, those words, are all we have, they are all we have access to on this side of the language barrier. Yeltsin may well speak right 'through' an interpreter, but all we have to make sense of are the interpreter's words. Nevertheless we say that Yeltsin declared so-and-so, that we have read Dostoevsky. Even though it is precisely the authoritative originary voice that is absent, we casually declare it is the only one that presents itself to us.

We feel we can be casual about this because we construe translation as a form of delegated speech, a kind of speaking by proxy. This implies not only a consonance of voices, but also a hierarchical relationship between them, and a clear ethical — often even a legal — imperative, that of the translator's discretion and non-interference. The imperative has been formulated as the 'honest spokesperson' or the 'true interpreter' norm, which calls on the translator simply and accurately to re-state the original, the whole original and nothing but the original (Harris, 1990).[4] The model of translation is here direct quotation: the translator's words appear within quotation marks because they are someone else's words, which are presented to us with minimal mediation. Although the translator speaks, it is not the translator who speaks. Translators, like their products, become transparent, spirit themselves away in the interests of the original's integrity and authority. Only the translator who operates with self-effacing discretion can be trusted not to violate the original. Transparency guarantees integrity, consonance, equivalence.

Now, the norms concept is there to remind us, forcefully, that what I have been describing — in the form of a caricature, perhaps, but not by much — is an illusion, a supreme fiction. We all know that a translation cannot coincide with its source. It contains different words, different meanings. Not only the language changes with translation, so does the enunciation, the intent, the moment, the function, the context. The translator's intervention cannot be erased without erasing the translation itself. Translation is necessarily hybrid, overdetermined, opaque, different. The belief in equivalence is an illusion — a pragmatically and socially necessary illusion perhaps, but an illusion nevertheless. And whatever is taken to constitute equivalence at one level, however measured, is offset by non-equivalence at other levels. Which leaves us with having to explain a paradox: if translation cannot undo difference, why is it that the presumption of equivalence has become so deeply ingrained in our standard concepts of translation? The notion of a 'translator function' may provide an answer.

The Translator Function

In the last 30 years or so, literary theory has had repercussions throughout the humanities. Among many other things, it has emphasised the role of the reader in investing texts with meaning, and highlighted the role of convention and intertextuality in the production of texts that are themselves variations on existing texts. As a result, we have come to appreciate not only the inexhaustibility and irrepressibility of meaning, but also, at the same time, the various conventional and normative mechanisms by means of which we have attempted to control this proliferation of meaning.

In 'The Death of the Author' Roland Barthes proposed that a text should be seen not as the sovereign creation of some Author-God but as 'a tissue of quotations drawn from the innumerable centres of culture' (Barthes, 1977: 146). When readers interpret texts they set them against this backdrop of known words and phrases, existing statements, familiar conventions, anterior texts. The meaning of a text is what individual readers extract from it, not what a supreme Author put in. Barthes' essay concludes by declaring that 'the birth of the reader must be at the cost of the death of the Author' (Barthes, 1977: 148).

Michel Foucault's essay 'What is an Author?' continues this line of thought by enquiring into the historical construction of the concept of 'the author' and its role in relation to questions of knowledge and power. Claiming that the concept of the author is 'a certain functional principle by which, in our culture, one limits, excludes, and chooses; in short, by which one impedes the free circulation, the free manipulation, the free composition, decomposition, and recomposition of fiction' (Foucault, 1979: 159), he posits the concept of the 'author function' as the ideological figure that our culture has devised to keep the potentially unbounded proliferation of meaning within bounds. We do this primarily by insisting on the author as a single unifying subject, with a single voice, behind the text. We thus suppress the more uncontrollable aspects of texts, their inflationary semantics, their explosive potential for interpretation, their plurality and heterogeneity.

Now, as especially Karin Littau (1993, 1997) has argued, translation constantly pushes in precisely the direction which the 'author function' was designed to block. Translations compound and intensify the refractory increase in voices, perspectives and meanings, they simultaneously displace and transform texts, and produce interpretations which, as verbal artifacts, are themselves open to interpretation even as they claim to speak for their originals. If, then, our culture needed an 'author function' to control the semantic potential and plurality of texts, it is not hard to see why it has also, emphatically, created what we might call a 'translator function' in an effort to contain the exponential increase in signification and plurivocality which translation brings about.[5]

As an ideological and historical construct, the 'translator function' serves to keep translation in a safe place, locked in a hierarchical order, conceptualised and policed as derivative, delegated speech. The metaphors and oppositions by means of which we traditionally define translation, the expectations we bring to translated texts, the self-images that translators themselves hold up, the legal constraints under which translation nowadays operates, all accord with this function. Because we know translation is strictly, normatively controlled, we feel entitled, against our better judgement, to override its inherent difference and presume equivalence. And so we say we read Dostoevsky, or Boethius. Just as we commonly accept that the most reliable translation is an 'authorised' translation, the one formally approved and legally endorsed by the author. The term itself confirms the singularity of intent, the coincidence of voice, the illusion of equivalence and, of course, the unmistakable relation of power and authority. The translator may claim authorship of the target text's words, but we want the original author to authorise them.

Historically this hierarchical positioning of originals versus translations has been expressed in terms of a number of stereotyped oppositions such as those between creative versus derivative work, primary versus secondary, unique versus repeatable, art versus craft, authority versus obedience, freedom versus constraint, speaking in one's own name versus speaking for someone else. In each instance it is translation which is subordinated, circumscribed, contained, controlled. And in case we imagine that these are after all natural and necessary hierarchies, it will be useful to remember that our culture has often construed gender distinctions in terms of strikingly similar oppositions of creative versus reproductive, original versus derivative, active versus passive, dominant versus subservient. The point I want to make in this connection is not just that the historical discourse on translation is sexist in casting translation in the role of maidservant, faithful and obedient wife, or '*belle infidèle*', or that it puts women in their place by confining them to silence or translation. It is that translation has been hedged in by means of hierarchies strongly reminiscent of those employed to maintain sexual power relations. It is worth asking whose interests are being served by these hierarchies.

It may well be, then, that the common perception of translation is that of an operation which produces equivalence, whatever the actual textual outcome. But it is a perception which privileges equivalence at the cost of suppressing difference. The interesting thing about the norms concept, and the issue of value raised by it, is that it invites us not only to recognise the primacy of difference but also to seek to explain the tenacity of equivalence. Let me add, for clarity's sake, that I do not think it necessarily follows from these remarks that translators should opt for different ways of translating. To my mind, the critical task of translation theory does not consist in advocating this or that 'resistant' — or, for that matter, compliant or 'fluent' or whatever — mode of translation. It consists, rather, in theorising the historical contingency of these modes together with the concepts and discourses which legitimise them. The primary task of the study of translation is not to seek to interfere directly with the practice of translation by laying down rules or norms, but to try to account for what happens on the ground, including the ways in which translation has been conceptualised. To the extent however that the historical discourse on translation blends into the contemporary scholarly discourse, our speaking about translation has to develop a self-reflexive and self-critical dimension. That takes me to my final point.

Translating Translation

There is one further, awkward complication to which I would like to draw attention. The essence of it was very neatly put by Quentin Skinner in the essay 'Conventions and the Understanding of Speech Acts' (1970). Skinner is here addressing the problem of how to assess the 'illocutionary force' of statements made by someone in a different context and not intended for us. The problem, Skinner says, is relevant to historians and anthropologists, who 'overhear' utterances produced by others for others. We can represent it as involving a person A, at a time and/or place t2, who is trying to make sense of an utterance by a speaker S who was speaking at t1. As Skinner points out, the problem 'is neither philosophically trivial in itself, nor in the practice of these disciplines can it be readily overcome' (Skinner, 1970: 136). Of course, A has to know enough about the concepts and conventions available to S at t1 so that A can grasp the semantics of S's utterance and what force S's enunciation of that utterance must have registered when it was uttered. But in addition, '... it also seems indispensable that A should be capable of performing some act of *translation* of the concepts and conventions employed by S at t1 into terms which are familiar at t2 to A himself, not to mention others to whom A at t2 may wish to communicate his understanding' (Skinner, 1970: 136, emphasis added, TH).

In other words, if we want to understand what Boethius intended to say, when we moderns 'overhear' his *De consolatione philosophiae*, we have to know something about the conventions of Boethius' time and place to grasp both the meaning of his words and the force registered by his uttering those words in those circumstances. It is worth remembering that this 'knowing' on our part is already a construction, determined by our perception and our conceptual categories. In addition however — and this is the main point — we need to be able to *translate* Boethius' concepts and conventions into our modern terms, especially if we wish to talk or write about our understanding of Boethius. So what if the object of our attention is not Boethius but a translation of Boethius? If we want to understand de Buck's translation of Boethius and communicate about it, we not only need to have a sense of de Buck's concepts and of his practice of translation, we also need to be able to *translate* his concepts and practice of translation into our translational concepts. To understand and speak about someone else's translation, we must translate that translation. When we want to understand someone's discourse about translation, we have to translate that discourse and the concept of translation to which it refers. Our accounts of translation constitute themselves a form of translation.

Two things follow from this. First, if descriptions of translation are performing the operations they are simultaneously trying to describe, the distinction between object-level and meta-level is rendered problematic. Descriptive translation studies in particular have been keen to keep object-level and meta-level well apart, but it turns out the object constantly contaminates its description.[6] Even the scholarly study of translation is implicated in the self-description of translation as a cultural construct. There is a worm in the bud of descriptive translation studies and their claim to disciplinary rigour.

Secondly — and here the norms aspect comes back into the picture — in translating other people's concepts of translation (or whatever term they use which we reckon we can translate as 'translation'), our accounts are unlikely to hold up a transparent image. They must be based on concepts of translation. As we saw, precisely because translation is norm-governed and impregnated with values, it is never diaphanous, never innocent or transparent or pure, never without its own intermingled voices. On the contrary, it appropriates, trans-forms, deflects and dislocates everything within its grasp. To the extent, then, that our descriptions amount to translations of practices and concepts of translation, they are subject to all the manipulations that come with translation. The nature and the direction of these manipulations are themselves socially conditioned and hence significant for what they tell us about the individuals and communities performing the translative operation, i.e. about ourselves. The study of translation continually rebounds on our own categories and assump-tions, our own modes of conceptualising and translating translation.

This is not new. Like other branches of the human sciences which cannot escape entanglement in the objects they describe, the discourse about translation, too, is obliged to render concepts and practices of 'translation' into its own terms. The issue becomes acute, however, as soon as we move beyond our immediate horizon. It surfaces whenever we wish to speak about 'translation' generally, as a transhistorical or transcultural phenomenon, or when we attempt to compre-hend and convey what another, especially a distant culture means by whatever terms they use to denote an activity or product that appears to translate as our 'translation'.

Since we cannot step outside ourselves or do without interpretation, there are no ready solutions to this epistemological paradox. But there may be ways of coming to terms with it. Luhmann's system theory may be one of them, if only because Luhmann is very conscious of the fact that observers cannot at one and the same time observe an object *and* their own observation of it. But let me look in another direction, one which is closer to the world of translation and which will lead us back to the notion of norms.

It is perhaps in cases where cultural differences are particularly stark that the issues come to the fore most clearly. That is why we may be able to learn most from a discipline like anthropology. After all, Edmund Leach recognised back in 1973 that for ethnography and anthropology 'the essential problem is one of translation', adding optimistically that 'social anthropologists are engaged in establishing a methodology for the translation of cultural language' (Leach, 1973: 772). They found that establishing such a methodology was rather more problematical that they may have imagined.

The complexity of the task can be illustrated with reference to a single (abbreviated) example. Early in the twentieth century Christian missionaries who lived for many years among the Nuer of the southern Sudan had concluded that the Nuer possessed a concept of 'religious belief' basically similar to or at least not wholly incompatible with what Westerners would designate as 'religious belief'. It is not unreasonable to think that perhaps the missionaries' assumption of translatability, which assimilated the Nuer conceptual world to their own, also facilitated the missionary endeavour itself. The observer's agenda may, consciously or unconsciously, have affected the observation by suggesting self-fulfilling presuppositions. When subsequently the Oxford ethnographer Edward Evans-Pritchard studied the Nuer in the 1940s and 1950s, he emphasised the utter otherness of the Nuer concepts and beliefs, their incompatibility with Western, Christian terms (Evans-Pritchard, 1956). He therefore highlighted the fundamental and formidable problem of understanding and interpreting, let alone of rendering, something which is alien but (presumably, hopefully) approachable through patient 'contextual interpretation', of rendering *that* in a language like English, i.e. in terms that are familiar to us linguistically and culturally, and therefore in terms that are always already tainted by our concepts, our history, our values. It was Evans-Pritchard who, in a lecture of 1951, described the central task of ethnography as 'the translation of culture' (Needham, 1978: 8).

An extended reflection on the linguistic, anthropological and epistemological problems connected with the 'translation of culture' is presented in Rodney Needham's *Belief, Language, and Experience* (1972), which patiently traces Evans-Pritchard's account of Nuer beliefs. Needham points out, for example, that, if we want to compare the German missionaries' interpretation of the Nuer terms with Evans-Pritchard's, we need to assess what 'adjustments' of Nuer, English and German were required to make the Nuer terms acceptable in the other two languages. When we know from what perspective and with what intention certain Nuer terms were bent or nudged in the direction of the other languages, we get an idea on what basis translation was considered feasible. We could then ascertain the ground on which comparability, commensurability and hence translatability had been constructed. But as Needham (1972: 222) also shows, there is no ideal metalanguage to carry out such a comparison. Such a language could only be constructed on the basis of the comparability of cultural concepts, but the concepts can only be compared on the basis of an already existing ideal metalanguage. That is a vicious circle. We cannot escape from perspectival observation, from value-ridden interpretation, from always-already-compromised translation.

Still, what Evans-Pritchard called 'contextual interpretation' can guard against the danger of rashly, reductively translating another culture's concepts into our terms. I assume Clifford Geertz (1983) has something similar in mind when he stresses the need for the anthropologist's 'participatory' practice as a way of gaining insight from within the culture in question. Speaking in the broader context of the social sciences Craig Calhoun recently argued that social theory should recognise the cultural construction of putatively general categories, pointing out that cross-cultural understanding involves translation problems in the attempt to grasp 'linguistic meanings which are not simply different from our own, but involve incommensurable practices' (Calhoun, 1992: 253). He then went on, however, to argue that translation is perhaps not a good description of cross-cultural understanding, as the latter is a process which must actually change the observer, enabling him or her to play both incompatible cultural games simultaneously without translating the rules and practices of one into those of the other (Calhoun, 1992: 256).

While Calhoun's point about the social construction of putatively general categories pinpoints the issue, I must say that I do not see how translation can be avoided in the context of cross-cultural understanding, especially if, in addition to gaining some private understanding, researchers wish to report back on their fieldwork to their own communities. Perhaps we can participate in Nambikwara life until we have become one of them, but only on condition that we resolve to live among the Nambikwara and never return — as indeed Jean de Léry recognised four hundred years ago in the (fictitious) colloquy written 'in the savage language and in French' which he inserted into his (very real) *History of a Voyage to the Land of Brazil* of 1578 (Léry (ed.), 1990, chapter XX; Pagden, 1993: 46–47).

If translation cannot be written out of cross-cultural understanding and description, then it matters that translation is governed by, and saturated with, norms and values. And here the somewhat more charged terminology which Eric Cheyfitz employs in his *Poetics of Imperialism* (1991) proves illuminating. Cheyfitz takes his time to explore the entanglement of translation with metaphor. This is more than just a fortuitous etymological link. Accounts of metaphorical language have traditionally been based on the distinction between the 'normality' of literal, proper, legitimate usage versus the figurative, improper, deviant, illegitimate, foreign, alien, 'abnormal' usage characteristic of metaphor (Cheyfitz, 1991: 88–121). Translation appropriates the foreign, normalises the abnormal and brands the illegitimate and the improper in the proper words of our own language. Cheyfitz then goes on to consider the translation of the North American Indians into the conceptual system of the early European explorers and settlers — and not only into the Europeans' conceptual, symbolic system, but also, in the same move, into their very material property system. Writing the Indians into a European context, mapping them onto the European world, means re-figuring and translating the other into our schemes. Given the power relations that are involved, it also means imposing our terms and categories. Nowhere is this historically more evident than in the very definition of the other as 'savage', as one who lacks something essential and valuable that we possess and he or she ought also to possess but does not, or possesses in some improper, perverse way which must be put right — whether it be script or scripture, fixed dwellings, certain moral standards or forms of social organisation, or indeed clothes or breeches. Faced with the radically different, we construe commensurability by translating on and into our terms. And our terms are not neutral but conditioned. And they cannot be reduced to a matter of equivalence, linguistic or otherwise.

When we engage in historical and cross-cultural studies of translation, we translate other people's concepts and practices of translation on the basis of our own, historical, concept of translation, including its normative aspect and the values it secures. We have no other choice. But having become conscious of the problem inherent in our descriptions we can devise strategies that acknowledge as much. That ought to be part of the ethos of the discipline. In this respect too we can learn from other areas of study. In recent decades ethnographers have become acutely aware of their discipline's roots in colonial history and of its present-day entanglement in structures of power and domination. As a result, ethnography has become markedly more self-reflexive and self-critical, aware of its own historicity and institutional position, of its presuppositions and blind spots, of the pitfalls of representation by means of language and translation. In the study of translation we ignore these issues and debates at our peril. It should be part of the critical practice of our discipline to acknowledge the normativity of our own representations of translation, and thus to make manifest the conditioning of our translation of translation.

Notes

1. Boethius' *De consolatione philosophiae* had been translated in the Northern Netherlands by the independently-minded D.V. Coornhert (1522–90), who saw himself as a universal Christian. Coornhert's translation appeared in Leiden in 1585 and was reprinted in Amsterdam in 1616 and 1630. A year after de Buck's 1653 translation Coornhert's version was reissued in revised form by François van Hoogstraten, an Erasmian with Catholic sympathies (Dordrecht 1654, 1655). De Buck's assessment is therefore broadly correct.
2. As far as I am aware Poltermann (1992) was among the first to apply Luhmann's system concept to norms and translation. See also Hermans (1997) and forthcoming.
3. Approaches to literature making use of the ideas of Luhmann and Bourdieu are discussed in the special issue 'The Study of Literature and Culture: Systems and Fields' of the *Canadian Review of Comparative Literature* (Van Gorp *et al.*, 1997). Gouanvic (1997) and Simeoni (1998) have applied Bourdieu's concepts to translation.
4. Speaking of interpreters, Harris posits the existence of a 'fundamental and universal' norm, which he calls 'the "true interpreter" norm, or ... the norm of the "honest spokesperson"'. He goes on to explain that 'this norm requires that people who speak on behalf of others, interpreters among them, re-express the original speakers' ideas and manner of expressing them as accurately as possible and without significant omissions, and not mix them up with their own ideas and expressions. Occasionally this norm is made explicit, as in the oaths which court interpreters have to swear under some jurisdictions' (Harris, 1990: 118).
5. Myriam Díaz-Diocaretz (1985) also speaks of a 'translator-function', but without explicitly basing her usage of the term on Foucault; see also Robinson (1997: 61–77). Rosemary Arrojo (1997: 31), too, has recently spoken of a 'translator function' with explicit reference to Foucault.
6. As far as I am aware, Bakker (1995), arguing from a Deconstructionist angle, was the first to draw attention to this.

References

Arrojo, R. (1997) The 'death' of the author and the limits of the translator's invisibility. In M. Snell-Hornby *et al.* (eds) *Translation as Intercultural Communication* (pp. 21–32). Amsterdam and Philadelphia: Benjamins.

Baker, M. (1998) Norms. In M. Baker (ed.) *Routledge Encyclopedia of Translation Studies* (pp. 163–5). London and New York: Routledge.

Bakker, M. (1995) Metasprong en wetenschap: een kwestie van discipline. In D. Delabastita and T. Hermans (eds) *Vertalen historisch bezien* (pp. 141–62). 's-Gravenhage: Bibliographia Neerlandica.

Barthes, R. (1977) The death of the author [1968]. In *Image, Music, Text* (Stephen Heath, trans.) (pp. 142–8). London: Fontana.

Bourdieu, P. (1994) *Raisons pratiques. Sur la théorie de l'action*. Paris: Seuil.

Bourdieu, P. (1996) *The Rules of Art. Genesis and Structure of the Literary Field* (Susan Emanuel, trans.). Cambridge: Polity.

Buck, A. de (1653) *Troost-Medecijne-wynckel der zedighe wysheyt ... Door ... Boethius ... Nu vertaelt ... door F.D. Adrianus de Buck*. Bruges: Lucas van den Kerchove.

Calhoun , C. (1992) Culture, history and the problem of specificity in social theory. In S. Seidman and D.G. Wagner (eds) *Postmodernism and Social Theory* (pp. 244–88). Oxford and Cambridge, MA: Blackwell.

Cheyfitz, E. (1991) *The Poetics of Imperialism. Translation and Colonization from The Tempest to Tarzan*. New York and Oxford: Oxford University Press.

Díaz-Diocaretz, M. (1985) *Translating Poetic Discourse. Questions on Feminist Strategies in Adrienne Rich*. Amsterdam and Philadelphia: Benjamins.

Evans-Pritchard. E.E. (1956) *Nuer Religion*. New York and Oxford: Oxford University Press.

Foucault, M. (1979) What is an author (Josué Harari, trans.). In J. Harari (ed.) *Textual Strategies. Perspectives in Post-structuralist Criticism* (pp. 141–60). London: Methuen.

Geertz, C. (1983) Art as a cultural system. In C. Geertz (ed.) *Local Knowledge. Essays in Interpretive Anthropology*. London: Fontana (1993).

Gorp, H. van, *et al.* (1997) The study of literature and culture: Systems and fields. Special issue, *Canadian Review of Comparative Literature* 24, 1.

Gouanvic, J.-M. (1997) Translation and the shape of things to come. *The Translator* 3, 125–52.

Harris, B. (1990) Norms in interpretation. *Target* 2, 115–19.

Hermans, T. (ed.) (1996a) *Door eenen engen hals. Nederlandse beschouwingen over vertalen 1550–1670*. The Hague: Bibliographia Neerlandica.

Hermans, T. (1996b) Norms and the determination of translation: A theoretical framework. In R. Álvarez and M.C.-Á. Vidal (eds) *Translation, Power, Subversion* (pp. 25–51). Clevedon: Multilingual Matters.

Hermans, T. (1997) Translation as institution. In M. Snell-Hornby *et al.* (eds) *Translation as Intercultural Communication* (pp. 3–20). Amsterdam and Philadelphia: Benjamins.

Hermans, T. (forthcoming) The production and reproduction of translation. System theory and historical context. Proceedings of the conference held in Istanbul, October 1996.

Hoven, R. (1997) De constantia. In F. de Nave (ed.) *Justus Lipsius (1547–1606) en het Plantijnse huis* (pp. 75–81). Antwerp: Museum Plantin-Moretus.

Leach, E. (1973) Ourselves and others. *The Times Literary Supplement*, 6 July 1973, 772.

Lefevere, A. (1992) *Translation, Rewriting, and the Manipulation of Literature*. London and New York: Routledge.

Léry, J. de. (ed.) (1990) *History of a Voyage to the Land of Brazil* (1578) (Janet Whatley, trans.). Berkeley: University of California Press.

Lewis, D. (1969) *Convention. A Philosophical Study*. Cambridge, MA: Harvard University Press.

Littau, K. (1993) Intertextuality and translation: *The Waste Land* in French and German. In C. Picken (ed.) *Translation: The Vital Link* (pp. 63–9). London: Chameleon.

Littau, K. (1997) Translation in the age of postmodern production: From text to intertext to hypertext. *Forum for Modern Language Studies* 33, 81–96.

Luhmann, N. (1984) *Soziale Systeme. Grundriß einer allgemeinen Theorie*. Frankfurt: Suhrkamp. (English translation: *Social Systems* (John Bednarz Jr., trans.). Stanford: Stanford University Press (1995).

Luhmann, N. (1986) Das Kunstwerk und die Selbstreproduktion der Kunst. In H.U. Gumpert and K.L. Pfeiffer (eds) *Stil. Geschichte und Funktionen eines kultur wissen schaftlichen Diskurselements* (pp. 620–72). Frankfurt: Suhrkamp.

Luhmann, N. (1990) Weltkunst. In N. Luhmann, F.D. Bunsen and D. Baecker, *Unbeobachtbare Welt. Über Kunst und Architektur* (pp. 7–45). Bielefeld: Cordula Haux.

Merton, T. (1973) The normative structure of science (1942). In N.W. Storer (ed.) *The Sociology of Science. Theoretical and Empirical Investigations* (pp. 267–78). Chicago and London: Chicago University Press.

Needham, R. (1972) *Belief, Language, and Experience.* Oxford: Oxford University Press.

Needham, R. (1978) *Essential Perplexities.* Oxford: Oxford University Press.

Niranjana, T. (1992) *Siting Translation. History, Poststructuralism and the Colonial Context.* Berkeley: University of California Press.

Pagden, A. (1993) *European Encounters with the New World. From Renaissance to Romanticism.* New Haven and London: Yale University Press.

Poltermann, A. (1992) Normen des literarischen Übersetzens im System der Literatur. In H. Kittel (ed.) *Geschichte, System, Literarische Übersetzung/Histories, Systems, Literary Translations* (pp. 5–31). Berlin: Erich Schmidt.

Pym, A. (1995) European translation studies, Une science qui dérange', and why equivalence needn't be a dirty word. *TTR* 8, 153–76.

Robinson, D. (1997) *What is Translation? Centrifugal Theories, Critical Interventions.* Kent and London: Kent State University Press.

Simeoni, D. (1998) The pivotal status of the translator's habitus. *Target* 10, 1–39.

Skinner, Q. (1970) Conventions and the understanding of speech acts. *The Philosophical Quarterly* 70, 118–38.

Toury, G. (1995) *Descriptive Translation Studies and Beyond.* Amsterdam and Philadelphia: Benjamins.

The Second Debate

The Notion of Equivalence

Peter Newmark (University of Surrey): I think that all translation is approximate, and by this you can mean rough, or you can mean as close as possible. When one says that one is aiming to find an equivalent, what all translators do, then I see nothing wrong with this. The attempt to dismiss this, which was first made by Mary Snell-Hornby about ten years ago, and now again by Theo, is misjudged. I think it is perverse to start with the difference as opposed to the equivalence. This may be interesting, but I do not think that it can be done seriously. There is a difference in literary and non-literary translation. Literary translation is more multi-factorial, or pluri-factorial, compared with the translation of facts. Nevertheless, the idea of accuracy still applies to both types of translation. This is what one is aiming at. Such remarks as 'translation tells us more about the translator than about the source language text' are, in my opinion, perverse. To me, translation is a noble activity, a truth-seeking activity — there are martyrs of translation. I worry about cynical attitudes toward translation.

Gideon Toury (Tel Aviv University): When Theo was speaking against the notion of equivalence, he was in fact speaking against *my* notion of equivalence, which means he actually spoke against a notion which defines the relationship between a translation and a source text as one which is defined as appropriate by the norms. I do not assume that Theo objects to the concept of there being any relationship between translations and source texts. I think that he would agree that not only are there such relationships, and that part of our research is to find out what they are. Moreover, it is a cultural and a scientific assumption that some relationship exists, and that there is a reason to look for it, although such a relationship cannot be defined in essentialist terms. The other question is whether this relationship should be called 'equivalence' or not. Theo, you say the term might lead the reader or listener astray who has got used to a different type of concept, covered also by the label 'equivalence'. I agree that there are advantages and disadvantages in redefining existing terms. In my opinion the advantages outweigh the disadvantages, whereas you highlight the disadvantages. What surprises me is that whereas I am at least consistent in my decision, I think you are not. You want to do away with 'equivalence' because the concept is defined differently, but you do not want to do away with the term 'translation'.

Theo Hermans (University College London): I do not disagree with your line of reasoning. However, I am arguing that when a culture regards a particular text as a translation of another text and then uses the concept of equivalence to describe that relation, and when you then as an observer and researcher adopt the same term, you destroy the possibility of distance. I think your deliberate decision to keep the term equivalence, even as a redefined term, is unfortunate. To me the disadvantage is that you adopt the term which is used in the field itself, and then re-use it as a term in translation studies, knowing that it is problematical.

Gideon Toury: Why do you keep using the term 'translation'? You are also using a term that is used in the field itself.

Theo Hermans: Because there I have no other choice.

Gideon Toury: Oh well, I think you do, as much as I have had a choice and could have decided to call the relationship by another name. Let us replace the terms by numbers, '111' is the relationship, and '000' is the entity. They are not overladen with any previous connotations.

Theo Hermans: That is not a realistic alternative.

Gideon Toury: I know it is not, and I know I am pushing things to the extreme. But I do not see a basic difference between deciding to retain the name 'translation' on the one hand, and retaining the name 'equivalence' but changing the concept on the other hand. I think it is not consistent to reject the one and retain the other.

Christina Schäffner (Aston University): The term 'equivalence' has always caused heated arguments. Linguistic approaches normally defined it as a relation between source text and target text which is based on an identity of meaning, and when we do not have this identity, then the texts would not come under the cover term 'translation', but would have to be called adaptation, for example. Within functionalist approaches, the notion is rejected, with the same argument Theo gave. But we still have some kind of relation between source text and target text, and when we want to describe it we need some name. The problem won't go away.

Peter Newmark: Isn't this purely playing with words? Equivalence means 'approximate', as all translation is, it does not mean 'exact'. Translation is always an essay, an attempt. The fact that there is no correct or perfect translation, that there are only various translations, shows that one is trying to reach the truth. And that's as far as one can go in another culture.

Theo Hermans: I think the reason why I hang on to translation but prefer to distance myself from equivalence, is that equivalence is a much more ideologically loaded word.

Peter Newmark: What do you mean by ideologically here? Which ideology?

Theo Hermans: The whole ideology that resides in the way we explain relationships between texts in translation studies.

Peter Newmark: Is it colonialist? Is it imperialist? I think it's quite the opposite, it's equality, it's democratic.

Theo Hermans: Well, think of it this way: We all say happily 'I have read Dostoevsky' or 'Yeltsin said so and so on television', and yet what we read or heard were not the words that Yeltsin spoke or Dostoevsky wrote. We feel entitled to use the shorthand, i.e. saying 'I have read Dostoevsky' and meaning 'what I have read is practically as good as Dostoevsky', precisely because we associate translation with equivalence, and with transparency. My point is that that is precisely a way of obscuring difference. We say for example, we have translated an Indian novel and here is its English equivalent, when in fact we have altered and transposed it to a different world altogether. There are power relations involved, and they are not relations of symmetry, sameness, or equality. Hence my unhappiness with the term equivalence. That is why I am interested in the question of why this term is there in translation in the first place, when we know that what happens in translation is approximate at best. Yet it is the approximation, the non-equivalence, which we obscure by saying 'it is equivalent, it is the same'.

Peter Newmark: Your difference question is often what translation theory is indeed interested in. The main point is that translation, in its democratic sense, has extraordinary power to produce friendship. This is what translation is all about, which you do not seem to recognise. With the increase of languages and the necessity of translation, this is a powerful instrument for friendship and peace.

Theo Hermans: I am interested in translation because it is a powerful instrument, not only of friendship and peace, but also of a lot of other things.

Peter Newmark: But this is its most important function.

Theo Hermans: I know it is. Already Goethe said so, and plenty of influential scholars. But translation is also an exceedingly complicated and paradoxical phenomenon. That is why it requires serious attention, and also political attention, attention to the implications of the terms in which we speak about it.

Gideon Toury: Do not forget that most of the terms used in translation studies throughout the ages were imported from other disciplines. Up till now, translation studies was annexed to other disciplines and it applied the terms that were typical of these respective disciplines. And to a large extent, this is still the case today.

Theo Hermans: This is also reflected in the way in which translators, throughout the ages, have described themselves, for example as servants, as subservient. And there again, I want to know why they do that, where that idea came from.

Kirsten Malmkjær (University of Cambridge): I think that the term 'equivalence' is problematic in the same way as the term 'identity' is. If you want a proper definition of identity, then you can use the one philosophers give, i.e. they see it as that relation in which something only stands to itself. You say that a text is equivalent to another one in the sense of taking them as being identical. Concerning my own research, I must say that I have been very much influenced by Gideon's brilliant re-definition of equivalence from an ideal to something you can find in the text. You can work very well with such a notion of translational equivalence, but of course you have to say at the beginning of your papers how you understand it. I think that when you read a translation of Dostoevsky it tells you something both about the translator and about Dostoevsky. The reason that you can say that it tells you something about the translator is because you can see the difference, that is when you are able to read both texts. The problem is that you have to talk about those two texts by using some sort of language. You can only say that the two texts are different from each other because you have a notion that they could have been the same. I do not see how you can talk about difference without equivalence. It is an interesting discussion to reflect about which terms to use, but I think it doesn't take us very far.

Theo Hermans: Although I questioned the wisdom of Gideon's decision to hang on to the notion of equivalence, I have not proposed an alternative. So what I am interested in, is reminding people of the fact that it is a problematical notion. I have no idea what other notion may be more suitable. Any notion which would be proposed as a replacement of the term equivalence would be beset by the same problems.

Peter Newmark: All translation is approximate. Why not just say that one is going for an approximation of equivalence?

Theo Hermans: I would prefer 'representation' in this case, which again does not solve the problems. And whatever we think Dostoevsky wrote in Russian is also our interpretation. When we comment on the relationship between the two texts, all we have to start with is the two texts. Whatever difference or similarity or approximation we bring out, is created in the writing of it. It is not given, we put it in.

Kirsten Malmkjær: But you have exactly the same problem when you are talking to people about some topic and realise that they do not share the background knowledge with you. Why can't we just accept some terms even if they are problematic?

Theo Hermans: Then you do what Gideon does. He is aware of the problems, and then he says you have to stop the discussion at some point and get on with research programmes. I want to linger on the conceptual problems, because I think they matter. They matter because they are ideological problems, loaded problems.

Kirsten Malmkjær: I think you should accept the fact that you do not get an exact equivalent and then go on. Those phenomena are fascinating, and we can see the value of relationships, but I think we should encapsulate all the difficulties and then move on to specific research projects, although I do accept the problematics that is there in translation studies, in philosophy, and so on.

Theo Hermans: I tend to think that both the history of translation and the current perception of translation are what they are precisely because these problems are not recognised.

Kirsten Malmkjær: But I also think that when you move on and set about some research project, you may find something that then casts doubts on the problematics with which you started.

Translation, Interpretation, Manipulation

Peter Bush (The British Centre for Literary Translation, University of East Anglia): It seems to me that all translation is interpretation, and it's inevitable and legitimate that it is interpretation.

Peter Newmark: Sorry, would you say that literary translation is interpretation? Surely factual translation is not.

Peter Bush: Well, I think actually that for translation of philosophy, history, sociological texts, political texts, it is. Perhaps in some legal texts, computer manuals and so on, there is less room for subjectivity or interpretation, but there is interpretation as well, decisions have to be taken. Let me talk about a translation that I was involved in. At the end of 1992 I went to Cuba to begin work on a television documentary on a director called Tomás Gutiérrez Alea. There I met a writer called Senel Paz who had written a short story about the relationship between a young communist militant and a gay intellectual. Alea was about to make a film about this and Senel had written the screenplay. The film was to become 'Strawberry and Chocolate'. Later on I went back to make a documentary, while 'Strawberry and Chocolate' was being filmed. Between those two visits I translated the short story which was published in the UK. During the filming of the documentary I could see the terrific tensions surrounding the history of oppression of gays under the Castro government. There were all kinds of tensions involved in making this film. In the end there was quite a lot of difference between the original screenplay and the final film. Our documentary came out on Channel Four before the film was shown in Cuba. I also became conscious during the filming of the documentary that there were certain questions that you could not ask people, or which they would not answer, because of the political situation. When the film came out, it was attacked by a professor of Spanish at Cambridge as being an anti-gay film. I was already negotiating with Bloomsbury to translate the original screenplay. I then took the decision to go back to Cuba and interview the author about the film, and take in the criticism which had been raised by leading gay critics here and in Germany. One of these criticisms was that the gay intellectual as portrayed in the film was too camp, that he was a stereotype of gayness. The film was actually about tolerance. I decided that I wanted my translation to be part of the debate, and to frame my translation with an interview with the author. I chose to translate the book in a certain way. When I read Theo's paper, I was struck by what he said about De Buck and the way that his translation had an ideological purpose behind it. It seems to me that it is perfectly legitimate that translators can have conscious strategies about what they are doing. They inevitably and consciously interpret what they are translating. It seems to me that the very notion of equivalence is a blunt instrument with which to analyse these complexities. You can't get into any of these cultural, social, and historical relationships if you are just talking about equivalence. Nida's theory of dynamic equivalence is rooted in his missionary work, and you can only understand how it functions in terms of his being a biblical translator.

Peter Newmark: I am sorry, but this is incorrect. The theory of dynamic equivalence which is now called functional equivalence precedes Nida. Many translators would agree with the idea that in ideal circumstances one should try and get the same reaction from the reader of the translation as one gets from the reader of the original. This has nothing to do with biblical translation. Nida goes beyond that.

Peter Bush: My difficulty with the terminology is Theo's use of the word 'manipulation', a word which goes back to the idea of translation being betrayal. I can understand that translation is for peace and friendship, and that translators also translate on behalf of fascist dictators, but why use the word 'manipulative' which is very loaded with negative resonances?

Theo Hermans: The reason why I still like it is that apart from being interpretation it also happens that translation is often deliberately manipulative. For example, there is manipulation in translations of English detective novels during the Nazi period, both in the selection of the books which were translated and in the way they were translated. Manipulation is an extension of interpretation.

Peter Newmark: But why tar this noble profession with this kind of example?

Theo Hermans: Because it is also an aspect of the profession.

Peter Newmark: In that case you could also say that medicine is manipulative because of what Mengele and others did in concentration camps. You cannot do that!

Said Faiq (Salford University): I agree with Peter Newmark, that translation as an activity of moving something from one culture to another, is something noble. Without it, we might never have encountered the great cultural changes and shifts from one civilisation to another. But when it comes to the actual act of translation then power relationships come in. Any translation act begins with the choice of the source text, and normally one translates texts that sell for one's own target readership, texts that your publishers would agree with. If we take this in the terms of equivalence, then equivalence should be looked for in the eyes of the readership, or in the eyes of the translator. I am glad that equivalence as a notion is in circulation, and that there isn't one single definition. It causes problems that are indeed important in translation studies and in the way we translate. And we have to deal with those problems.

Theo Hermans: I have no quarrel with that at all. I only want to remind myself and others that in order to do justice to the complexity of translation and the many — noble and ignoble — uses of translation, we must remain critical of our own terms. And 'equivalence', I think, precisely because it looks so innocent, is a term from which we must keep our distance. I haven't proposed another word for it. 'Representation' or 'rewriting' may be possible, but they are so broad.

Said Faiq: We could use the Arabic equivalent for 'equivalence' which literally means the existence of the two. In the western tradition of translation and the definition of equivalence within the English language there is the idea that one starts with a source but then the source disappears and the transparency takes over.

Gunilla Anderman (University of Surrey): Yesterday, when we were talking about what *Hamlet* meant, I was waiting for somebody to make the point that in all likelihood Shakespeare himself did not know what *Hamlet* meant. Anyone who has attempted to translate a writer and has asked the writer 'what did you mean?' may get the answer 'I do not know what I meant'. This is because there are certain types of analysis which actually hinder rather than help certain forms of creative expression. That means that translation must be interpretive, and must lend itself to the types of manipulation that we have been talking about. Interpretation is really inevitable, it must be there. We can't forgo that notion.

Theo Hermans: This only restates the ubiquity of interpretation. But interpretation is not innocent, it comes from somewhere and it serves a purpose.

Gunilla Anderman: Sure, for example Oscar Wilde was reinterpreted and made presentable for German readers during the Third Reich.

Translation as a Specific Kind of Communication

Alexandra Lianeri (Warwick University): I am not sure about the relation between translation and interpretation, that is, whether translation presupposes interpretation or whether it is identical to it. Let us say that interpretation is based on our conceptual and cultural presuppositions as well as ideological perspectives. I then wonder whether translation should be considered as a form of appropriation of the source text, which is confined to the already existing conceptual capacities of the target culture, without having the potential of transforming them. On the other hand, can we extend the notion of interpretation, by describing it as a process which underlies both interlingual/intercultural and intralingual/intracultural communication? In this case we can do away with a binary dichotomy between source text and translation, and describe the reception of the source text as a chain of interpretations within the target culture. Yet, how would it then be methodologically feasible to establish the difference between translation, as a conscious attempt to rewrite and represent 'otherness', and intracultural interpretation?

Theo Hermans: Understanding otherness involves a form of appropriation, in a sense that you can only project onto what you observe elsewhere from your own standpoint.

Alexandra Lianeri: I accept this. My question was whether a notion of appropriation implies that one should consider the conceptual capacities of the target culture as static and limited, or whether one could argue that the conceptual and cultural framework of the target society can be altered through the import and rewriting of a source text.

Theo Hermans: I suppose it can only be altered on certain conditions. The conditions would be that the kind of difference which the importation of that other product makes, can only be one which is compatible with the prevailing conditions in the target culture. For example, when the Europeans went to the Americas they described social structures among the native American Indians. But of course they did so in terms of kingdom, tribe, nation, freedom, and in terms of property relations. Whatever difference translating texts from that world could have made in Europe could only have occurred on condition that the terms on which a translation took place were compatible with what was there in Europe. In other words, it may have been possible, for example, for a group of people in Europe who thought of setting up a Utopian society, to read what they saw in North America as providing a possible model for them. Whatever social structure they saw among the native Indians, they would still interpret in their own terms, appropriate it within their own context. We only understand others in our own terms, and if we import ideas or concepts, it is on our conditions. There was a strong awareness during the Renaissance, that when people were translating from Latin or Greek their vernacular was hopelessly inadequate. Latin was the language of intellectual discourse, it had a copious vocabulary to deal with ethics, philosophy, botany, and so on. So what the translators did was to import neologisms from Latin, to create new words on Latin models, and to create new words out of existing roots. In some cases this worked, in others it didn't. But in each case, the difference which was made could only be made and be successful to the extent that local conditions were perceived to be compatible. That's how translations can make a difference.

Alexandra Lianeri: The conceptual framework of the target culture should then not be defined either as static or as closed but one can consider that it can potentially alter through translation. If we then come back to what I have said earlier regarding inter- and intralingual communication, do you think that we can distinguish between translation, as a means through which the target community defines the linguistic and cultural limits of the 'self' in opposition to 'otherness', and intralingual, or more accurately, intracultural communication, i.e. communication within these limits? Would you agree that if one argues for a dispersal of any distinction between translation as representation of 'otherness' and intracultural interpretation, then any form of communication would be defined as translation, so that it would be impossible to define any methodological boundaries between translation theory and communication studies?

Theo Hermans: There is no doubt that there is an element of translation in all communication, and George Steiner illustrates this beautifully in the first chapter of *After Babel*. There have also been arguments against that view. They came from philosophers who said that we do assume, rightly or wrongly, that when we speak we understand one another. This assumption may be false, but you can only try to substantiate it by arguing further about it, i.e. by communicating, and trying to figure out if you are being understood. I think that the only practical solution is to say that we live in a culture where there is a concept of translation. We, as scholars in translation, may want to keep our distance from it, so that we can look at it, but we cannot step outside it. From a semiotic point of view, Jakobson's argument in 1959 that there are three types of translation, i.e. interlingual, intralingual and intersemiotic, may be logical. At the same time we know that the person in the street does not think of translation in these broad terms. All we can do is bear in mind that there may be a semiotic logic that says that you cannot really distinguish and that there is an element of translation in all communication, but we know simultaneously, that translation, as most people outside this room would use it, does mean interlingual translation, and only that. This is also why I venture this definition of translation as a verbal representation of an anterior text across an intelligibility barrier, which is that kind of semiotic idea. It does not exclude Jakobson's intralingual translation, but then intralingual means to the extent that, for example, I cannot understand the Glaswegian dialect. I would rather speak of intelligibility barriers instead of languages to avoid the idea of languages as neatly delineated entities.

Loredana Polezzi (Warwick University): I do not disagree with what you just said about 'interlingual' and 'intralingual', but I find it difficult to reconcile with what you said before, namely that you think rewriting is too loose a term. What you have said just now fits in with a definition of translation as rewriting.

Theo Hermans: The definition as I gave it in my paper came in two stages. A verbal representation of an anterior text, and typically such a form of representation that it can or will be accepted as a re-enactment of the anterior text. And not all forms of rewriting are re-enacting.

Loredana Polezzi: I agree, not all rewriting is re-enacting, but some forms are.

There is not such a neat boundary. What I am more interested in is how what you have been saying relates to the question of what translation studies does and what it is. It seems that what you have been saying about how the target culture and the source culture interact and how they are called into question by what happens in translation, somehow creates, or requires a new space for a translation studies which is not target oriented, but which looks at interactions between target and source. I think your paper calls into question the whole idea of description. You say at the end that description itself is a kind of representation and interpretation and that this is quite legitimate and unavoidable. If that is the case, we also need to be critical and look back at the idea of translation studies as descriptive translation studies. I read what you are saying as going forward toward a self-reflective, or a critical practice as an integral part of research in translation studies. Is this correct?

Theo Hermans: Yes that is quite right. Concerning the target orientedness, I would say that the important thing is not to take the target-oriented nature of the descriptive studies that Gideon and others promote and turn it into a dogma. The reason why it was put forward originally in the 1970s, and why it was quite forcefully promoted, was to counter the predominant source-oriented, prescriptive, normative kind of translation studies. The target-orientedness was also based on the assumption that when translation happens it is more likely that the answers to why certain things happen and not others, are probably to be found on the translator's side. All the relevant answers to translational questions are in the target culture. As regards descriptive studies, what I am trying to do is to highlight a problem, which in other disciplines has been highlighted before. When we realise that when we describe we also translate translations, we are the fly in the ointment of descriptive translation studies. What that statement says is that the object contaminates the describer or the description. That is what makes me sceptical of some of the scientistic jargon that I detect in Gideon's writing, for example, the attempt to be neutral, objective, to stand outside, which I think is undermined by this kind of reflection. Gideon might say that you can recognise the problems but then you have to move on. And he is right, of course. But you only get on in a more self-critical mood when you acknowledge that there is a problem there. Translation description is already contaminated by the object that it tries to describe: we describe translation, but we can only do so on the basis of a concept of translation. This concept is not innocent, neither are our descriptions. It's a bit like interpretation. You cannot get away from it but you can be aware of it and you can look at how other disciplines, like anthropology or sociology, have tried to come to terms with it.

Transparency, Sameness and Difference

Myriam Salama-Carr (Salford University): I am interested in transparency because it seems that we are talking of two different levels there. One is rather abstract in that we can work on the premises that translation is not transparent because of the norms that bear upon the work of the translator. However, there is also the fact that a translation can appear to be transparent although it probably involves as much interpretation and perhaps even more manipulation than a translation which we see as non-transparent. Would it be useful to distinguish between those two levels? I think it might be, because when we speak of transparency we often think of the translation as a text, for example we find a non-domesticated translation that conveys quite a lot about the source culture and the source language.

Theo Hermans: Are you using transparency in the way that Lawrence Venuti would use fluency? When I use transparency, I mean basically all translation. Maybe the way to approach it is to take translation as a form of delegated speech. The translator is a sort of relay station, and gives us what we cannot get direct access to. I don't have access to Dostoevsky because I don't speak Russian, that's why I read a translation. And I like to think that what I get is Dostoevsky. If I want to keep alive the illusion that I am reading Dostoevsky, then I must close my mind to the whole dimension of translation. I know, deep down, that there was an intervention, but I would like the translation to give me a direct, transparent view of the original, without any intermediary. That is what I mean by transparency. To that extent I construe transparency as part of the ideology of translation.

Gunilla Anderman: You seem to answer the question 'Why do we want to believe in transparency?' with 'because we want to believe in illusions'. I was linking that to the idea of equivalence, where you suggest we start from difference, as opposed to sameness. Some of us seem to have difficulties with that, and I think that it may have something to do with the idea that as children we do start assuming sameness. A child is totally narcissistic and as it grows up it comes to realise that there are differences. But most people still assume sameness, and therefore it is only people who are in a situation in which they combine two cultures permanently, who are aware of the fact that one might possibly start from difference, but that is an acquired awareness. I think perhaps that the idea of starting from sameness is more intuitive whereas starting with difference is counter-intuitive if you are monocultural.

Theo Hermans: I quite agree, except with your conclusion. When we communicate we do not quite know whether we are on the same wavelength as the other person, but we assume we are. Pragmatically we must assume things such as equivalence, transparency and so on. That is the way we organise our loyalties. The point is this: when I speak, a lot of the things I say are not grammatical, or do not follow from what was said before, and yet you manage to filter out all this and focus on the main points. What needs explaining about this process is what Luhmann calls the improbability of communication, the fact that it appears to work despite the improbability of it ever succeeding. It seems to me that if we want to study translation, it is precisely the counter-intuitiveness of difference which is a good way in, so as to unhinge the obviousness of translation. That is also the reason why I harp on this question of equivalence. Gideon, who is extremely critical of equivalence, has built up an argument and provided a new definition of the term whereas I question the wisdom of sticking to it, because it means that you work within the terms already given within the field itself.

Gunilla Anderman: That makes entering into your way of thinking difficult for a lot of people.

Theo Hermans: That's too bad!

Peter Newmark: Do you yourself ever review or examine translation work? I'm asking this because if you do, is it not a very negative approach to start with where a translation fails, in other words, stressing the differences between the translation and the original? If you do this with students then, I think, they will be very depressed. Surely the opposite would be more encouraging for a student, and would be a more optimistic approach, because you show how translation works and succeeds.

Margaret Rogers (University of Surrey): Are we talking about different purposes here? Surely we should distinguish something which we use as a research method from something which we use as a technique in the classroom. If you take an analogy from psycholinguistics, we learn a lot about the successful production of speech by the way speech breaks down under certain conditions of anxiety, tiredness, etc. It seems to me that there is a parallel here. You said that as a method of investigating translation you wanted to unhinge the obviousness of translation, and in the same way if you unhinge the obviousness of the way we speak you can actually find out more about what is going on in a system when it breaks down, than when it succeeds. It seems to me that what you are arguing is a method of research but not necessarily something that we would do in the classroom.

Theo Hermans: I do review translations. I am involved in a course that is meant to provide students with training in literary translation, and I also translate myself. What I think I gain from approaching things through difference rather than sameness is the fact that every translation involves already as a starting point a text which is different and which you know you are not going to recreate as it is, because the language in which you work is different, the context is different, the purpose for which you provide the translation is different from the purpose for which the source text was provided. In the context of translation, difference is given much more immediately than sameness. To speak about translation in terms of sameness is upholding an ideology of translation as it has existed for some centuries. The reason why I start from difference, also in the work with my students, is that I want to make them aware of the fact that what they are doing is not to try to recreate but to provide, for a particular purpose and for a particular audience, a text which the receiving audience will — hopefully — accept as a representation, or a re-enactment, of a source text. So difference has nothing to do with errors or with making mistakes, but it has to do with the historicity of translation.

Peter Newmark: Surely the translator is trying to empathise with the writer, and what you say seems to be denying this very obvious fact if one is talking about literary translation. You seem to be exaggerating the time difference of people too. I am also worried by your repeated use of the word 'innocence'. It is always used in a negative sense. There are many more things to translation.

Theo Hermans: Sure, there are many more things, but the things that I like to focus on are the things that you sweep under the carpet.

Peter Newmark: I think of translation as a truth-seeking activity.

Peter Bush: It seems to me that the current ethical approach to translation within translator training, this critical consciousness, is essential, because without a critical consciousness of difference and one's own relationship to difference one cannot critically examine one's own translation through the numerous drafts as you approach an interpretation.

How to Get from Micro-level Text Elements to Norms

Abdulla Al-Harrasi (Aston University): We have been talking about the concept of norms at a more general level. I am interested in the practical application, that is the question of how we can make use of the concept of norms as a research tool in translation studies, particularly for studying more specific phenomena as, in my own research, metaphors.

Gideon Toury: If you want to study one linguistic phenomenon in one source text and its translations, I wonder whether the best tool, methodologically speaking, would be the notion of norm, especially if you do not know the behaviour of metaphors under translation in any other texts. There is a danger that you pretend to work on one text while actually you are taking into account what you know about the behaviour in other texts as well. It is risky to work with such a notion because you would assume that any regularities you find are caused by norms, because that is what you are looking for. Norms are not phenomena which only influence one translator while translating one text, much less so one translator while translating one type of phenomenon in one text. If you do not have a corrective mechanism, you have to be very cautious. You can only say this is one possible hypothesis, but it will have to be put in a much wider context in order to be verified, modified, or refuted.

Abdulla Al-Harrasi: Do we go from the specific to the general, or vice versa?

Gideon Toury: You can go both ways, but it depends on what you understand by going from the specific to the general. Would more general mean more translators dealing with the problem of metaphor, or would it mean metaphor plus something else? There are several ways of enlarging the corpus.

Peter Newmark: It seems to me that if you were to take twenty typical metaphors in one language, for example 'carrying coals to Newcastle', and show that this is translated into German as *'Eulen nach Athen tragen'*, that is 'carrying owls to Athens', that appears to me to be the norm. You do some research on it and show that both these metaphors are 'frothy', and make a critical comment on it. You do this with twenty metaphors and I think that might be a useful research job.

Said Faiq: It seems that if we can bridge the gap between norms and strategies, we may end up with certain ways of changing values of certain norms. Theo spoke of value transformation, and Peter Newmark listed a number of ways of handling metaphors in translation. In Arabic, 'carrying coals to Newcastle' would be selling water in an area where there are a lot of water sellers.

Gideon Toury: But I am not sure that it will be translated that way all the time. This is the real question, and not what you would regard as the *best* solution. We should ask what translators actually do, and I am not sure they will always use the same phrase in their target texts.

Said Faiq: But if a norm is established, it would act as a guideline.

Beverly Adab (Aston University): I am getting confused now between norms and strategies. I thought that norms were tendencies which dictated types of strategies, but not necessarily particular strategies.

Gideon Toury: I do not think that there is a gap between strategy and norm, they do not belong to the same set of terms at all.

Beverly Adab: When you talk about 'carrying coals to Newcastle', Peter said the norm is that it is translated by a certain phrase. To me, this would be a frequently employed strategy rather than a norm, and the norm would be to try to find an equivalent idiomatic expression. The norm tells you the type of behaviour but not the actual instance of the behaviour.

Gideon Toury: The norm is the idea behind it. The way you carry it out involves strategies.

Beverly Adab: But if we conflate the two terms 'norm' and 'strategy', we will have more confusion. And I just wondered if Peter's example was a good example.

Gideon Toury: It could end up being a good example of norm if you really came up with a bilingual concordance of the actual replacements of this particular English idiom. If you study its behaviour under translation in 200 different texts, and half of them are literary and half of them are non-literary texts, and half of each type of text are from the eighteenth century and the other halves from the twentieth century, then you might end up finding patterns which could lead to the extraction of norms.

Theo Hermans: I think that one way of solving the question of whether a frequently used strategy can be called norm is to talk about norms in terms of expectations: what you know as a translator what the audience expects from you, and what the audience knows that you as a translator expect from them.

Gideon Toury: Let's stick to metaphors. Many people have found out that there were languages and cultures, and especially literatures of different periods of time which simply hated metaphorical terms. If they translated texts from other languages which had metaphors in them, they ended up with translations which did not have metaphors. And this happened not because metaphors wouldn't have been available, but simply because the norm of this particular period was against too flowery a style.

Beverly Adab: But you have taken it up a level anyway, which was what I was trying to argue. You are talking about metaphors, not about one particular metaphor. I don't think you can actually apply the concept of norm to a particular strategy with one particular utterance which is actually idiomatic.

Gideon Toury: It would not be incorrect, but it would be a sort of misuse, because if everything is guided by norms then the notion of norm loses its force as an analytical or descriptive tool.

Kirsten Malmkjær: I think that metaphors are quite difficult to identify, and the methods for translating them may differ from metaphor to metaphor. Several students where I work, have done something similar, although not with metaphors, but with other micro-textual features. One Japanese student looked at how sentence final particles were translated because there isn't an English category which corresponds to that category in Japanese. You get guidelines in grammar books about what to do, which you might take as norms. She looked at actual texts to see how those items had been dealt with in the translations. Once she had identified the ways they had been translated into English, she looked for these features in other texts in order to see whether they were in fact translations. It does give you an interesting perspective on what grammar books say, compared to what translators actually do.

Gideon Toury: I think that the most significant point of what you said is the conclusion that translators often do things that are not in the textbooks. A couple of years ago we had an article in the journal *Target* on the translation of passives from English into Arabic. The authors took an English text with some passive forms and gave it to a group of students and a group of professors of Arabic and had them translate the text. Then they analysed the replacements of the passive forms, and what they found was a greater variety than in any book. They also found interesting patterns. This is another example of the kind of analysis you can do on the micro level. But because the corpus was not big enough any assumptions about norms would have been premature.

Beverly Adab: But when you have a large and well defined corpus, couldn't you then use this corpus to study and extrapolate the norms from it?

Gideon Toury: The problem is that there is something circular here. You assume right from the start that the translation of, let's say, metaphors is dominated by norms, and that if you look hard enough you will find them. But there is no way of really verifying your findings.

Theo Hermans: The difficulty arises because of the fact that you can observe regularities and you can see that someone has made a particular decision, but that does not tell you why the translator made that decision. One would need to ask not only why the translator chose a particular option, but also what other options were available, and why they were not chosen. You can only begin to answer that by opening up the field of vision, the corpus, and bring in the social, ideological, historical and other factors. So it may depend on how the translator assesses the relevance and difference of metaphors in, for instance, Arabic political discourse. It may depend on how other political speeches, that is non-translated political speeches in English, carry metaphors. It may depend on the translation tradition, or how they are taught translation. You can't decide until you have explored all these possibilities.

Gideon Toury: It may also depend on the target audience.

Loredana Polezzi: Putting the findings of a micro-level analysis into the larger social, historical, ideological context is very important. If you only list the regularities that you discovered in a corpus and say that this is how it is done, then there is the risk of becoming prescriptive. But by historicising your findings you avoid this risk.

Margaret Rogers: It seems to be useful to have a control corpus as well. In this way you can compare the translated texts with originally occurring texts, so that you can look at the way the features you are studying do or do not occur in your control corpus.

Translation, Norms and Sanctions

Jean-Pierre Mailhac (Salford University): Theo said that one of the important dimensions of the idea of norm was a sanction as being linked to it. Assuming you find a pattern of regularities looking at metaphors, what kind of sanction could be associated with that, and how do you identify this? And if there is no sanction, are we then dealing only with regularities but not with a norm?

Theo Hermans: The sanction could be quite immediate, of course, in that the translator could lose his or her job. It could also be that the sanction is not really visible, in the immediate sense, but the translator might not get another contract. It could also be that a particular translator is complimented on the excellence of a translation. That is a form of sanction as well, albeit a positive sanction, in terms of praise and perhaps more money for the translator.

Jean-Pierre Mailhac: In terms of a specific research project, these are putative sanctions. Presumably there will not be any evidence of real, positive or negative sanctions linked specifically to the particular data of let's say again the translation of metaphors. Are you then still talking about norms, or do you have to talk about regularities, because all you have is totally fictitious and putative sanctions, for which you have no real evidence.

Theo Hermans: In a case like that you cannot know. It is probably not this or that particular metaphor that gets singled out for praise or criticism. Sometimes it is possible to isolate a particular micro-textual aspect to an overall general reaction, but in many cases it will not be possible to do so. However, reviewers or readers frequently react to the translations of novels and other works, commenting on clumsy style, for example. These are also a type of sanction, indicating the sort of expectations that audiences have when they are confronted with translated texts.

Jean-Pierre Mailhac: Methodologically you are not uncomfortable with the idea of the term 'norm' being applied when the sanctions are not necessarily observable?

Theo Hermans: Not necessarily, no. Of course, if it turns out that you can never identify any sanctions at all, then you ought to rethink.

Peter Newmark: I think that the word sanction is being misused. I think positive sanction might work in another context, a context of punishment, imprisonment. But I couldn't understand the use of the word here. I would have thought that if the translation resulted in something in the wrong style or register, that would be a sanction against duty.

Said Faiq: You also have a duty with regard to your client. When it comes to translations of political discourse, then the general norm is that the translations into whatever language are normally official translations, institutionalised by the government. And even if an error is detected, nothing can be done about it, because it had already been made official.

Future Research Projects

Christina Schäffner: We have already touched on the question of how particular research projects could tell us more about norms in practice. It might be interesting to continue this debate and see whether we can identify a number of specific research projects we want to tackle.

Theo Hermans: Something which, as far as I know, has not yet been done is a study of the psychology of reading translations. How do we respond to translations when we come across something that seems to be incongruous or anomalous? Will it make us go back to the source text? What leads reviewers to give positive or negative comments on translations? I think we need studies on the reception of translations, on evaluative statements about translation, statement made both in the past and at present.

Gunilla Anderman: How could this be done? How could we measure the reaction of readers to translations?

Theo Hermans: Yesterday somebody mentioned that when you come across something which is unusual in an utterance by a native speaker, you may respond to it differently compared to when you come across the same utterance by a non-native speaker. In the one case you assume it is a creative usage, in the other case you assume it is an erroneous usage. It may well be that when we read translations, we do it in the same way. I would find it intriguing to study how people respond to what they perceive as errors in translation, and to know when somebody calls something an error in translation, on what grounds they justify doing so. It might tell us something about what is understood by translation.

Gunilla Anderman: So, for example, you could let people read and comment on a particular text and not reveal that it is a translation.

Theo Hermans: Yes, you could try that. It has been done, in fact, as a way of trying to test out the concept of equivalence.

Gideon Toury: It has been done before, and also my story about the three killers was precisely an exercise to make students aware that, without noticing it, they are applying norms. For methodical reasons, one would need a text which would make the right impressions.

Theo Hermans: The one case that I am thinking of is a study by Stegeman, called *Übersetzung und Leser* (1991). By means of questionnaires, he tried to study how people responded to a text in the original, and how they responded to various translations. The idea was that if you could verify that translation and original produced the same responses, then you could say that it is possible to measure equivalence in terms of readers' reactions, because different stimuli produced the same effect.

Gunilla Anderman: Would the difficulty then be to measure the responses?

Theo Hermans: I would think so, yes. Precisely how you would do that, I do not know because I am not a psychologist. But it seems to be one possible way forward to test attitudes toward expectations of translation. Another way would be to look at reviews of translations, responses to translation and so on, to see what precisely it is that is marked as good or bad in translations and find out on what grounds these value judgements are made.

Gunilla Anderman: This is what Vanderauwera did to a certain extent, when she measured the responses to Dutch literature in translation. What struck me there was the absence of positive comments. Pinpointing something negative is of course easier. This is why I asked about problems in measuring.

Gideon Toury: There is a methodological problem here as well, because there are norms and models of writing a review.

Lordana Polezzi: I know of at least one case in which the translation of an Italian book into English was praised for being much more readable than the original text. However, this positive appraisal of a translation is based on a negative perception of the original. The problem lies in controlling the many variables.

Christina Schäffner: It is also a problem in the methodology. When you tell people here is a translation and please tell me what you find strange in it, then you will surely get a whole list of presumably strange phenomena.

Gideon Toury: But if you do not tell them, they sometimes hit on certain phenomena and supply the hypotheses that it is a translation themselves, which is much more interesting.

Theo Hermans: We can also look at codes of conduct of translators' associations, or at the history of copyright law concerning translation. Not all that much has been done on it, as far as I know. But it would be interesting to study how it has grown, how it is justified, because copyright law encapsulates concepts of translation in particular societies.

Christina Schäffner: Codes of conduct are very much prescriptive. At the seminar we had here last year on translation and quality, we spoke about the standards that are appearing in different countries to use as quality assessment for professional translators. It would be an interesting exercise just to compare the standards that exist in various European countries in order to find out whether there is a general consensus concerning standard requirements for professional translators.

Theo Hermans: We can also look at laws which concern the accountability of translators. When a translator makes an error, what happens, who takes responsibility? I am sure that the discussions around these concepts lead you to concepts of translation, and to what individuals, communities, societies want from translation and how they want it to be carried out. This also takes us into the area of borderline cases, debates about what counts as a translation as opposed to adaptation or paraphrase. Any case where there is dispute can be quite revealing.

Gideon Toury: My favourite example is the phenomenon of fictitious translation. Sometimes a text may succeed in retaining the status of a translation and in being regarded as a translation for a rather long period of time, precisely because the author of the text knows what is typical of genuine translations in his or her own culture, and incorporates such phenomena normally associated with genuine translations in his or her original text.

Mark Shuttleworth (Leeds University): Do you mean linguistic phenomena? Or do you include in this phenomena which one might call translationese?

Gideon Toury: Yes, but not only those. Examples of translationese are very easy to find. I have studied a number of such fictitious translations in various cultures, and you can learn a lot about the cultural conception of what a typical translation is.

Said Faiq: Another interesting point is accountability. Gaddis Rose reports on the consequences of a poor translation that led to the death of a worker operating certain machinery in the Middle East. Who is to blame in this case, the translator or the translation agency for not having checked the text properly?

Theo Hermans: This also concerns the issue of what defines an error in translation, which is much less simple than it looks. It would depend on the nature of the contract as well. If the translator can show that s/he has worked to the best of his/her ability, s/he may not be held accountable.

Said Faiq: That is the common practice in a Western context, but the practice in the Arab world is different.

Theo Hermans: Then there is all the more reason to look at it. One can only appreciate what is specific to one case if one can see alternative solutions.

Said Faiq: I think one way to encourage this kind of study is to embark on collaborative research involving more than one area, particularly areas outside mainstream European translation theory and practice.

Theo Hermans: And we would also need interdisciplinary cooperation. For example, we need psychologists who can tell us how to set up a proper questionnaire, or when legal aspects are involved, we require lawyers from different traditions and different areas.

Peter Bush: There ought to be a research project on the publishing of translations and on the process of translation and rewriting drafts, and the ways these two interact. You mentioned contracts. Well, the standard contract for literary translation in the UK has just some rather general statement, saying that it should be a faithful translation and it should be in good literary English. I wonder how often that kind of clause is invoked between publishers and their translators. It would be interesting to go through publishers' archives and see how often there are legal issues between publishers and translators, for example because publishers introduced editorial changes in the translation without consulting the translator.

Gideon Toury: It depends on whether there is a clause in the contract saying something about the responsibility for editing. The standard contract in Israel says nothing about it, only that the publisher is entitled to make changes. But when I translate we add a clause saying that they are entitled to make changes, but I have to approve them.

Peter Newmark: This would be very difficult to do because I do not think many publishers would cooperate.

Peter Bush: Lawrence Venuti has done some research for which he got access to archives. One of the things the British Centre for Literary Translation is doing is to establish an archive of translations, manuscripts and so on. This would be a first step to approach publishers and get their cooperation.

Description, Explanation, Prediction: A Response to Gideon Toury and Theo Hermans

Andrew Chesterman
*Department of Romance Languages, University of Helsinki, Yliopistonkatu 3,
00014 Helsinki, Finland*

Norms

When norms entered Translation Studies, they offered solutions to two kinds of theoretical problems. First, they offered a way of escape from the tradition of prescriptive studies: much of the older thinking was prescriptive in tone and intent, with translators proposing general principles about what translations should be like, or appealing to such principles in justifying why they had translated the way they had. The concept of norms allows modern translation scholars to take a distance from this prescriptiveness: we can describe the norms which appear to exist in a given culture at a given time, but it is the norms that do the prescribing, not the scholars. That is, the norms are experienced by those who translate as being prescriptive, regulatory. To break these norms is to run the risk of criticism; but it may also, of course, lead to the establishment of new norms. As Toury stresses, norms are thus of central importance in the training of translators, in their socialisation into the profession.

Second, norms offered a way of explaining *why* translations have the form they do. Given certain features of a translation, or of translations in a particular culture at a particular period, we can propose norms as causes of these translation features, or of these translator's decisions: the translator did this, because he or she wished to conform to a given norm. In translation research, norms are thus not really ends in themselves, but means; they are explanatory hypotheses that may help us to understand more about the phenomenon of translation.

One major result of the introduction of translation norms has been the expansion of the object of study. We now have a wider concept of what translation is, and of what it can be, than earlier. The move from an essentialist position (a translation must have feature X) to a relativist one (let us see what kinds of texts are called translations in this culture) has been enormously beneficial here, in freeing research from unnecessary constraints. However, the essentialist position cannot be rejected entirely: there must be some constraints on what we take as translations, otherwise we might as well study any text at all, or even the universe in general. Toury himself (1995: 33–35) has proposed three postulates (that there is a source text, that there has been a transfer process, and that there is an accountable relationship between source and target) which look like conditions for a text to be called a translation, although he says that these postulates are not factual but indeed 'posited', to be tested against the data. If all three hold, we have good grounds for assuming that the text in question is indeed a translation — but it still might not be.

So norms are useful. But they do give rise to some conceptual problems of their own. I will just mention a couple here. Toury's understanding of norms is extremely broad. He sees the concept as covering a scale of constraints on behaviour (in section 3.8 of his paper), a scale which ranges from relatively absolute rules to pure idiosyncrasies (but nevertheless excluding conventions, which I find curious). Some norms are more rule-like, others are 'almost idiosyncratic'. Indeed, he goes so far as to say that rules and idiosyncrasies are in fact no more than 'variations of norms', so that rules are 'more objective norms' and idiosyncrasies are 'more subjective ones'. I wonder how helpful this is. Surely, norms by definition are social, they express social notions of correctness. They are intersubjective if they are anything. To claim that they can even cover (or nearly cover) subjective idiosyncrasies is to stretch the concept unduly. Let us not make it so general that is loses its usefulness.

Hermans' concept of norms extends from rules to conventions, which seems to me a better continuum than one including idiosyncrasies. But Hermans also extends the concept in a way that I think is misleading. He appears to see norms also 'as regularities of behaviour' (in sections 2 and 3). Toury (3.6) is careful to avoid this equation: the regularities themselves are not the norms, they are merely evidence of the norms. To confuse the two is a category mistake.

Hermans stresses the sense in which norms involve 'expectations about preferred options', and he also wishes to include, within his understanding of norms, the 'anticipation of expectations'. This seems to correspond to the distinction I have made between expectancy norms and professional norms (Chesterman, 1997: 64–70). Expectancy norms are the expectations of the target readership and the client etc., and the professional norms explain the translator's tendency to take account of these expectancy norms. By conforming to norms, translators also contribute themselves to the continuation and strengthening of the norms.

Some may feel that if we see translations as being subject to norms we deprive translators of their free choice, we reduce them to the status of mere rule-following robots: on this view, norm-thinking makes translation into a mechanistic, predetermined activity. Both Toury and Hermans reject this inference. Toury points out that although norm-breaking carries the risk of sanctions, the translator can always choose to act differently, provided that he or she accepts the responsibility for the consequences. You are free to break the norms, if you can get away with it — and maybe make new norms. Hermans highlights the fruitfulness (for scholars) of looking at alternatives which were available but which the translator chose not to take. Translators always have a choice.

Equivalence

Undermined by skopos theory on one side and by norms on the other, equivalence has been having a hard time recently. In the good old prescriptive days, of course, equivalence was at the centre of the essentialist definition of translation: a translation is a text that is equivalent to another text in another language. No equivalence? Not a translation. The effect of Toury's argument has been to shift equivalence from being an *a priori* requirement to being a result, a result of the translator's decisions. This text has been accepted in this culture as a translation (i.e. it evidently conforms to the norms), therefore it must bear some kind of relationship with its source — let's now see what this relation actually is; whatever it turns out to be, I will call it 'equivalence'. As well as extending the range of valid relations between source and target, this methodological procedure does certainly tend to make the concept of equivalence rather vacuous, as Hermans argues. Why not, indeed, focus on the difference that translation makes, rather than on an illusory preservation of sameness?

But do we have to make this binary choice? What about taking similarity as the key term: not sameness or difference alone, but *both* sameness *and* difference? After all, this is what 'similarity' means: partly the same, but partly different. In the process of translation, some aspects of the source text appear to change more than others.

Hermans wonders why equivalence has had such a long life in Translation Studies, and has not disappeared long ago. In the folk concept of translation, some such formulation as 'different language but same meaning' has surely always played a major part — but why? Hermans suggests a postmodern explanation: to control semantic diffusion, the infinitude of potential meanings. All right, but simpler explanations are also available, such as the need to trust a speaker of another language; the need to predict the behaviour of others; common sense, even. Consider an interpreter at an international meeting, or a bilingual guide helping a foreign client in a market-place. 'Trente francs' has to be 'thirty francs', not twenty.

Another reason for the survival of equivalence, suggested by Hermans, is that we tend to think of translation as a form of reported speech, in which the translator is relegated to a secondary position, merely representing the speech of someone else. The translator thus becomes 'invisible', transparent. Some recent work in Translation Studies has taken up this theme, and sought to propose ways of giving the translator more visibility. I wonder, though, whether this would best be done via the target text itself (translating in a 'visible' way), or by other extratextual means. I am not convinced that a translator's *textual* visibility is necessarily a desirable goal, certainly not for all kinds of texts. What about focusing on extratextual, sociological issues more, such as pay, working conditions, public image and status, professional organisations, etc.?

Explanation

Toury points out, and Hermans illustrates, that norms can provide explanatory hypotheses for characteristics of translations. Indeed, Toury even goes so far as to imply that since norms are explanatory hypotheses they are not really entities in their own right at all, which seems a bit extreme (3.6): if norms are social facts, they surely exist as social entities, not merely as a scholar's hypotheses?

Toury returns to his useful distinction between *acts* of translation and translation *events* (in 4.2). A translation act takes place at the cognitive level, and consists of the decisions that a translator makes, plus the various mental routines that maybe do not really feel like separate decisions. A translation event is something sociocultural: it comprises the various aspects of the communicative situation and the social background, the client etc., which impinge upon the act of translation. If we call the totality of a translation's linguistic features a *translation profile*, we thus have the following chain of causation:

Translation event —> Translation act —> Translation profile

If we ask why a translation profile has a given feature, we can first posit an initial cause — an explanation — in terms of the translation act: we find this feature, because of this decision, this translation strategy. If we then ask: why this decision, this strategy?, we can appeal first to the translator's state of belief and knowledge, part of which is his/her knowledge of the relevant translation norms and his/her attitude towards these norms. If we continue to ask why (why this belief, this attitude?), we have to go back further and look for causes in the sociocultural situation in which the translation was requested and carried out, including the norms themselves as social facts, plus such factors as the training and personal history of the translator, etc.

With this kind of conceptual picture, we can look for, propose and test no end of interesting hypotheses, some pertaining to the initial cognitive cause (e.g. in protocol studies) and others pertaining to the sociocultural causes lying behind these.

Values

Why do norms exist? Partly in order to make life easier, of course, because they help us to predict how people are going to behave, and help us to decide how we ourselves are going to behave. In other words, they exist to promote the values that permit social behaviour, such as trust. They also exist in order to promote other values, other ideologies. Hermans links this idea to the fact that translations are always different from their originals, and that it is precisely in this difference that the underlying value, or ideology, can be seen. He claims (at the end of section 2) that translations are always slanted representations, and that 'translations can never be value-free'. As such this claim is surely a platitude: after all, surely no human action is 'value-free', so how could translation be? The fact of inevitably reflecting values or ideologies does not depend on the fact of representing difference. Even a translation that was totally equivalent, with no differences at all (an impossibility, granted), would reflect values: viz. the values (and associated ideology) promoted by total equivalence. Transparency and ideological neutrality are also values, they are not 'value-free' concepts.

For Hermans, values thus appear to be associated with non-neutrality, with inevitable bias. Value, like meaning, is to be found in difference. In fact, for Hermans, we might even gloss 'value' as 'added or different meaning' (call this value-sense 1). It is this additional meaning that then reveals underlying ideological goals, the motives of the client and/or translator, power relations etc. (value-sense 2). For Toury, on the other hand, values seem to be rather different kinds of concepts (4.5). Values are the ends towards which social action is oriented (or, more modestly, the shapers of interactive tools). The value behind translation, Toury writes, consists of two major elements: producing a target text (a) which is designed to occupy a certain position in the target culture, and (b) which constitutes a representation of a source text. These 'values' seem more like functions to me (value-sense 3), although 'function' is also itself a slippery term.

It is clear that Hermans and Toury are not using the word 'value' consistently in anything like the same sense. Perhaps Translation Studies still needs some conceptual analysis on this point, in order to arrive at an agreed interpretation of this key concept (see e.g. Pym, 1997). Is this why Toury places the term in quotes in his heading to this section? Why then nevertheless prefer this term to 'function'?

Effects

Norms prescribe. Unlike the case with conventions, norm-breaking can lead to sanctions (or indeed rewards), evidenced in the reactions of readers and/or clients. By bringing norm theory into Translation Studies we are thus implicitly also focusing on the effects of translations as well as their causes. The initial effect of a norm-conforming translation is (normally) its acceptance, by client and readers, rather than its rejection. Clients and readers may refer to norms in order to justify their (perhaps intuitive) responses as to whether a given translation is 'good' or 'bad'. Teacher evaluations are similar instances of translation effects (effects on the teacher), as are judgements like 'this does not seem like a translation' or 'this is obviously a translation'. Toury points out that it is precisely via the internalisation of such 'environmental feedback' that translators learn the tricks and norms of the trade. His study of the reactions to the Hemingway story is also a kind of translation effect analysis.

The chain of causation can thus be extended forwards, as follows:

> … Translation profile —> Effect(s) on client/readers —> Effect(s) on target culture/on intercultural relations …

The effect on the client/reader is initially a cognitive one: we might even define 'initial effect', in a preliminary way, as a change of cognitive state. This change may in turn have behavioural or cultural or intercultural repercussions. The Manipulation School of translation research has stressed the power of translators to bring about effects of the latter kind, such as the creation or strengthening of national identity.

Just as we can make hypotheses about causes, we can also make hypotheses about effects: more precisely, we can venture predictions about them. Given a translation profile with a particular feature, for instance, I might predict that the effect (on the client/reader, or on the target culture eventually) will be such-and-such: e.g. that the client will think this is a bad translation. I might then utter a prescriptive statement: translators working on this kind of text should not do this — because their work will be rejected if they do. Or: translators with this kind of text should do that, not this. These statements are not then mere empty speculation; they are conclusions drawn from studying client/reader reactions, the effects of translations. The study of effects thus re-opens a space for prescriptive statements, provided that these are indeed justified by adequate evidence. To be sure, effects are not easy to define nor to measure: there is ample scope for basic research here, too.

Conversely, given such-and-such an effect, I might suggest a cause: it was because the translation profile was like this, which was in turn because of such-and-such antecedent conditions. This kind of research, proposing and testing hypotheses of cause and effect, may indicate a future course of empirical progress for Translation Studies.

Within Hermans' framework, translation effect analysis comes under the reception of translations. In the translator's head, the image of the potential effect/reception of the translation forms part of the translator's expectations about the target audience and their expectations. This image then plays a part in regulating the translator's decisions.

Toury's questions about the membership of the relevant group within which translation norms are negotiated (4.4) are highly relevant here. Scholars often tend to assume that the relevant group is mostly composed of scholars, and real-life clients are sometimes forgotten. The study of real-life effects has also been somewhat neglected: rather less energy has gone into this than, for instance, into the conceptual analysis of equivalence — of interest to scholars, perhaps, but of much less interest to clients and typical readers.

Strategies

Strategies are ways of responding to norms. Toury observes that Lörscher's analysis (1991) of translation strategies is pitched at the level of the translation act (the cognitive level), not at the sociocultural level of the translation event. (This may be one reason why Lörscher's typology has not been applied as widely as his actual definition of a strategy.) I agree that we need a broader understanding of what strategies are and how they might be classified. We might start by distinguishing between three types:

(a) linguistic strategies or shifts, at the level of the textlinguistic profile of the translation (such as transposition, paraphrase); these can be seen as text-producing processes or as the results of such processes, and are caused by
(b) psychological strategies like Lörscher's, at the cognitive decision-making level (ending with something like 'find and accept solution'); these in turn are partly caused by
(c) sociolinguistic behavioural strategies, at the level of the translation event, such as 'phone an expert, check an Internet source, compare with a parallel text'.

In principle at least, each of these strategies has its own particular effects. Hermans observes, for instance (in section 2), that using a paraphrase strategy means that the translator must speak 'more overtly in his or her own name'. This is, in fact, one effect of such a strategy — but it is an effect that will probably only be noticed by a scholar or critic who has the source text at hand to compare, for an ordinary reader (or client?) will not necessarily recognise a paraphrase as such. So we have a problem: if we study effects, on whom shall we study them? To what extent, and on what grounds, can we generalise from the effects that a given strategy has on a scholar or a critic? As Toury notes (4.10), a translation teacher may say that a given translation is good, but 'society' may not agree.

Theory

A final point that emerges from a comparative reading of these papers by

Toury and Hermans is their broad agreement on the goals of a translation theory. Toury distances himself from the view that teachers (and scholars) of translation are trying to change the state of the world: Translation Studies is not a form of social engineering. His emphasis is on descriptive-explanatory research rather than 'mere theorising' (paragraph 1). He goes on: 'For me, theory formation within Translation Studies has never been an end in itself. Its object has always been to lay a sound basis and supply an elaborate frame of reference for controllable studies into actual behaviour and its results and the ultimate test of theory is its capacity to do that service'.

By 'mere theorising' I take it that Toury means conceptual analysis, the fashioning and refining of conceptual tools that can then be used in proposing and testing hypotheses. True, tools are not fashioned or refined for their own sake; but we do need tools, they are not 'mere' tools. The purpose of a conceptual tool is to carry out some function, e.g. to aid understanding, or to bring an insight, or to make a useful distinction, or to propose a descriptive taxonomy or a framework for effect analysis, or to allow the formulation of a hypothesis. If a tool does not serve the function for which it was designed, or any other function, we can get rid of it. This may be the case with the concept of equivalence. On the other hand, for instance, Toury's conceptual distinction between the act of translation and the translation event is useful if it allows us to formulate testable explanatory hypotheses.

Hermans too rejects the view that translation scholars should themselves 'interfere with the practice of translation' or 'lay down rules or norms' (i.e. be prescriptive); instead we should seek to account for what happens when people translate, and also when people think about translation (e.g. folk concepts). His emphasis, though, appears to differ from Toury's in the status he gives to 'theorising': 'the critical task of translation theory', writes Hermans (at the end of section 6), 'consists in theorising the historical contingency of [different modes of translation] together with the concepts and discourses which legitimise them'. No 'mere theorising' here: to theorise is presumably to describe and explain — the general aims of any scientific discipline.

One problem with this view of the general descriptive and explanatory goal of Translation Studies is the distance between it and the expectations of professional translators, who would rather see the theory produce something which would be of direct relevance and use to them. In the eyes of professional translators, all too often, translation scholars give the impression of being engaged in an elaborate glass bead game in an ivory tower far from the nitty gritty of everyday translation problems.

I think there is a real danger here, that Translation Studies risks becoming too much of an inward-looking activity, a kind of mutual citation club, too concerned with its own status as an academic discipline and not concerned enough with the real problems at the messy grassroots of life in a big translation company, for instance. Hermans' metatheoretical worries about translating translation, about engaging in any discourse about the subject of translation because of the familiar but inescapable hermeneutic circle, seem light-years away from such real-life problems. Not that such worries are uninteresting — far from it. But what empirical consequences might they have? Yes, translation is saturated with norms and ideologies. Yes, Cheyfitz (1991), for instance, has pointed at some of the causes and effects of certain translation strategies in a particular context. So: should we translate differently? How? Examples? What would the effects of this different kind of translation be? How do you know? Evidence? Should we write differently about translation? How? Hermans suggests that scholars (and translators?) can 'devise strategies' that acknowledge the problems of talking about translation, the problems of acknowledging and representing difference. Can we? Evidence? Evidence that such strategies would have different, desired effects? Effects on society as a whole? On intercultural relations? On translators? On translation scholars?

References

Chesterman, A. (1997) *Memes of Translation*. Amsterdam and Philadelphia: Benjamins.

Cheyfitz, E. (1991) *The Poetics of Imperialism. Translation and Colonization from The Tempest to Tarzan*. Oxford: Oxford University Press.

Lörscher, W. (1991) *Translation Performance, Translation Process and Translation Strategies: A Psycholinguistic Investigation*. Tübingen: Narr.

Pym, A. (1997) *Pour une éthique du traducteur*. Arras: Artois Presses Université.

Toury, G. (1995) *Descriptive Translation Studies and Beyond*. Amsterdam and Philadelphia: Benjamins.

Norms in Research on Conference Interpreting: A Response to Theo Hermans and Gideon Toury

Daniel Gile
Université Lumière Lyon 2, 46, rue d'Alembert, 92190 Meudon, France

Introduction

When I was invited to write a contribution on the topic 'Translation and Norms', I hesitated. The mathematician in me likes the definition of translation as a function of norms in the relevant cultural space, and I have always felt that the use of the concept of norms in the scholarly study of literary translation was opening up new possibilities. However, my personal interest lies in scientific and technical translation and in conference interpreting, and I have always focused on topics in which either the norms were taken for granted and prescriptive (in the didactic field), or cognitive issues were at the centre of attention (in conference interpreting). Attempting to write a direct response to Theo Hermans' and Gideon Toury's statements would have been foolhardy. However, as regards my own field:

(1)   I have become convinced that norms must be taken on board when studying a number of issues in conference interpreting in which they have been ignored so far, including quality research and didactics.

(2)   I consider norm-related research into interpreting attractive as an avenue for new projects and believe it is likely to foster more empirical research into interpreting and more interdisciplinarity, in particular with sociology and with research on written translation.

(3)   As an analyst of research into interpreting, I feel that in the past decade or so, research in the field has been increasingly governed by status-oriented norms at the expense of problem-solving. Becoming aware of these norms and their operation is important for researchers in the field.

(4)   Very little has been written about norms in interpreting, so that even a text by a quasi-ignoramus may contribute something.

This text offers a few reflections on the role of norms and research on norms in the field of interpreting, and briefly refers to a case-study to show that norms should be taken on board in one type of empirical research in which they have been neglected so far.

Norms: A Neglected Factor in Interpreting Research

Much thought has been devoted to empirical investigation of interpreter performance under various conditions, from Barik (1969) and Gerver (1976) to Tommola and Laakso (1997). In most of these cases, performance assessment was based on a comparison of words or propositions in the source text and the target text without taking into account interpreting strategies: researchers considered that deviations from the source text in the target text were due to cognitive problems, without allowing for deliberate decisions by the interpreter to add this or omit that to improve the target text (for example Jones, 1997). Ironically, sometimes it is precisely when there is cognitive overload that the interpreter cannot implement such strategies and may be forced to render the source text literally without optimising it (as is illustrated at the end of this contribution). The implication is that the metric chosen by researchers who neglect such strategies may measure the opposite of what it is supposed to measure. A correct identification of norms is necessary in order to calibrate the propositional or other metrics used.

Interpreting strategies are at least partly norm-based just as translation strategies are, with one major difference, namely that in conference interpreting, many of them primarily address cognitive constraints. In Gile (1995a: 201–4), five 'rules' that could explain the selection of interpreting strategies are identified. Out of these, two are what could be called 'target-norms', namely 'maximising information recovery' and 'maximising the communication impact of the speech', and one is an 'optimisation norm', namely 'minimising recovery interference' (choosing a strategy that is less likely to cause problems with another speech segment). Actually, 'maximising the communication impact of the speech' can be considered a hypernorm covering norms such as 'making the meaning sufficiently clear', 'avoiding potentially offending translations', 'finishing one's interpretation as rapidly as possible' (for TV interpreting), 'in a setting with many non-native speakers of the target language, making one's language neutral' (avoiding typically American, British or Australian expressions in English, or Canadian or Swiss expressions in French) etc. As reflection and observation of field phenomena advance, other norms can be identified, listed and classified, depending on the context.

An interesting question for research is to what extent norms differ as one moves from the didactic environment to the professional environment, and from the interpreters to the users. A number of studies (in particular Kurz, 1996; Moser, 1997; Kopczynski, 1994) have shown that different user groups have different expectations from interpreting. Are interpreters aware of these norms? If so, are they taught in the respective training programmes? If not, when and how are they learned by the interpreters? One norm that was hammered into students at the interpreting training programme I attended in France insisted that interpreters were just that, and did not do any written translation in the framework of an interpreting contract. Reality turned out to be different. Following that norm and many others taught in school would have caused professional damage. How many norms have a similar destiny?

Fidelity norms are of paramount importance for research, but also for specific segments of the interpreting activity, in particular court interpreting (see Morris, 1993). Focusing on their importance in research, if they are not based on pure propositional matching between source text and target text, what *are* they based on? In a recent study, I found that assessors do not necessarily agree on what is and what is not an error or omission (Gile, forthcoming), but the actual criteria are virtually unexplored. Interestingly, while a prevailing norm in conference interpreting is the interpreter's 'neutrality', meaning s/he takes side with the speakers as they take the floor, one sign-language interpreter who attended an interpreting workshop told me she signed to her deaf clients not only *what* the speakers were saying, but also *about* the speakers, their style, their personality, etc. She was surprised that this was not the usual norm among conference interpreters. Other sign-language interpreters have not confirmed this as a usual norm among them. French sign-language interpreters have also told me that they disagree with the norms taught at the sign-language interpreting programme in one particular school in France. The issue is clearly of some importance and deserves to be investigated systematically.

In view of the on-site, on-line nature of interpretation, beyond linguistic output norms, the interpreter's behavioural norms are also an important area to investigate, especially in court interpreting, in business interpreting, in interpreting for health services, and in sign-language interpreting, but also in conference interpreting. Sociologically speaking, a number of phenomena would be particularly interesting to study, such as the norms adopted by interpreters under the pressure of time and action when interpreting speakers whose social status and behavioural and linguistic norms are different from their own: male/female, immigrant vs. native or adminstrative authority, young/old, low-class vs. high-class individual, etc. Working on norms could provide new insights into this aspect of the interpreting profession(s).

Research on Norms: An Attractive Avenue for New Projects

The cognitive paradigm that has become popular in research into interpreting over the past decade or so is not an easy one for beginners. Research on norms is more attractive insofar as it requires no experimental set-ups with or without inferential statistics and no acquisition of abstract, rather complicated knowledge on cognitive theories that seem remote from the act of interpreting. In a paper published ten years ago, Shlesinger was pessimistic about the possibilities, and focused on pinpointing 'those factors which encumber both the formation and the extrapolation of norms for interpretation' (Shlesinger, 1989: 111). Unlike her, I believe that in many countries, interpreters are exposed to the work of much more than a handful of colleagues, and that much is learned about norms in the course of initial training, where teachers are active professional interpreters and every student's performance is assessed and corrected orally and in public, as opposed to the correction of written translation assignments. Moreover, I believe that research about norms does not necessarily have to rely on large speech corpora. In the field of interpreting, such research is probably more efficiently done by asking interpreters about norms, by reading didactic, descriptive and narrative texts about interpreting (what Toury, 1995: 65 calls 'extratextual' sources), by analysing user responses, and by asking interpreters and non-interpreters to assess target texts and to comment on their fidelity and other characteristics using small corpora. The topic of norms and the corresponding research procedures may be more attractive to many than work on cognitive issues, as they are more closely related to actual interpretation work, and information collection is relatively easier and interesting on a professional level. An added advantage is the fact that the considerable amount of existing non-scholarly literature (for a list of published texts over the past eight years, see *The IR(TI)N Bulletin* issues 1 to 17), that has been of little interest to researchers so far except for some historical work, could be explored for norms and may yield new insights into the profession.

Work done on norms in interpreting could allow interesting interaction with work done on norms in written translation, where decisions and behaviour are essentially similar, but tend to occur under a lesser time pressure and off-site. On a different level, work on norms is likely to open up the researchers' mind to sociological concepts and working methods, which have been neglected in the field of conference interpreting. As explained below, this could have healthy paradigmatic implications as well.

Norms in Interpreting Research

Interpreting research is still very remote from actual applications. Even in the field of didactics, Dodds (1997: 90) rightly points out that 'many many more years of intense research' will be necessary before one reaches that stage. More significantly, for the time being, research in the field is not prevailingly oriented towards problem-solving, and seems more intent on improving its general methodological quality and on gaining scientific status (for example, Lambert & Moser-Mercer, 1994, the special issue of *Target* on Interpreting Research [7:1], Gambier *et al.*, 1997). This aspiration, associated with the attractiveness of the cognitive disciplines to investigators of conference interpreting, gives the hard-nosed experimental paradigm defended by some psychologists (but not all — see Gardner, 1985) excessive power and threatens further methodological development in the field: if you want to be 'scientific' and to be 'taken seriously', do 'serious' empirical work, preferably experimental, preferably with inferential statistics (Lambert, 1994: 6; Moser-Mercer, 1998: 42). Although I was trained in this paradigm and have been calling for empirical research alongside these and other researchers since the early eighties, I feel that such norms are dangerous and that openness in paradigmatic and methodological choice should be defended. Identifying and exposing prevailing norms and their sociological interaction in the field may help.

A Case Study

I should like to conclude with a concrete example to illustrate some of the ideas discussed above. The following data comes from a study on the variability of fidelity perception: quantitative comparisons were made as regards target-speech segments which were either reported or not reported as errors or omissions (e/o's) by various types of assessors, here professional interpreters (PI) vs. non-interpreters (NI), under visual (V) and auditory (A) presentation conditions (Gile, forthcoming). As will be understood, the findings suggested that qualitative studies of the phenomenon focusing on norms was called for. Source-speech extract:

> Hello Ladies and Gentlemen. I'd like to apologise for the the films they weren't very informative. But that wasn't my fault. It's because the Vietnamese government chopped out what I really wanted to show you. Anyway um there's one thing I'd like to correct and that is I'm down as the 'Brigade Foundation'. I am in fact the Christina Noble Rigade Foundation.

I say I called it 'Rig' because I was hoping to encourage the oil people to give a little bit back to the countries that they take the oil from.

Corresponding target-speech extract:

> *Bien. Bonjour mesdames et messieurs, je voudrais m'excuser pour les films qui n'étaient pas très informatifs. Ca n'était pas vraiment ma faute. Il y a eu des parties que le gouvernement vietnamien a censurées. C'étaient justement les choses que je voulais vous montrer les parties que je voulais vous montrer. Je voudrais simplement dire que je ne suis pas la fondation Brigade comme c'est écrit sur le papier mais je suis je représente la Fondation Rigade Christina Noble. J'ai parlé de Rig parce que j'espérais que les compagnies pétrolières rendraient quelque chose à ceux dont ils prennent le pétrole. Il y a un jeu de mots parce qu'en anglais le mot 'Rig' s'applique à l'infrastructure de l'exploitation pétrolière ... les machines.*

The data below represents the proportion of professional interpreters (PI) and non-interpreters (NI) who reported the particular segments selected here as errors or omissions:

Segment (1): The interpreter added emphasis when translating '... that wasn't my fault' by saying 'Ca n'était pas *vraiment* ma faute' ('It wasn't *really* my fault').

	PI	NI
A	0%	23%
V	21%	25%

Segment (2): The interpreter omitted the explanatory 'because' in his French translation of 'It's because the Vietnamese government ...'.

	PI	NI
A	0%	0%
V	14%	30%

Segment (3): The interpreter omitted the idea of 'correcting' in 'There's one thing I'd like to correct', and translated the verb by 'dire' ('say'):

	PI	NI
A	17%	20%
V	18%	30%

Segment (4): The interpreter replaced 'oil people' by 'compagnies pétrolières' ('oil companies').

	PI	NI
A	6%	13%
V	14%	10%

Segment (5): The interpreter omitted 'countries' (in 'to the countries that they take the oil from'). Instead, he referred to 'ceux dont ils prennent le pétrole' ('those that they take the oil from').

	PI	NI
A	17%	26%
V	21%	15%

The following comments can be made:

(1) The fact that segments were not reported as e/o's by all the assessors can be partly explained by attention fluctuations which caused subjects to 'miss' them, especially in the auditory mode where the information is either processed immediately or disappears from working memory (as is seen clearly in another study, where assessors missed such e/o's and imagined other e/o's — see Gile, 1995b). However, as demonstrated by comments some of the subjects made spontaneously (see below), part of the explanation probably lies in variability in their fidelity norms. One methodological challenge is to discriminate between 'non-reportings' made because of cognitive 'misses' and those made because of norm variability, just as it is important to ascertain the differences between fidelity norms for written texts vs. auditorily presented speeches. Without them, performance assessment may be too unreliable.

(2) Besides high variability in the number of e/o's reported in each group and each presentation modality, the study showed the lack of a clear correlation between the number of e/o's reported and the general fidelity rating given by the assessors for that particular target speech. On a scale of 1 (very poor) to 5 (very good), in the visual mode, fidelity ratings of 4 were given for 0, 1 and 2 e/o's, but also for 9 and 15 e/o's, and in the auditory mode, fidelity ratings of 5 were given for 0,1,2,3,4,5,6 and even 12 e/o's. On the other hand, three assessors out of four who reported no e/o's rated fidelity at 4, not 5. This last result suggests even more strongly that fidelity norms include a meaningful element other than clearly identifiable errors and omissions.

(3) The study was quantitative and not qualitative, and the subject of norms was not pursued further, but a few comments made by the assessors spontaneously will help illustrate norm-based variability. A few speculative comments were added by myself on the basis of my reactions as an assessor and a professional interpreter (I make no claims regarding these hypotheses, to be expanded and tested when the subject is taken up in a qualitative study).

In e/o (1), the addition of 'vraiment' ('really') in '... that wasn't my fault' was considered by some a 'natural' utterance *which did not add emphasis* despite the adverb (comments made by subjects).

In e/o (2), while some subjects may have missed 'because' due to insufficient attention, at least some of them considered that the context made the causal relationship between 'it wasn't my fault' and 'the Vietnamese government chopped out what I really wanted to show you' clear enough to make the word unnnecessary (comments made by subjects).

In e/o (3), the word 'correct' before a sentence correcting the name of the speaker's foundation may have been considered redundant in informational term by some respondents (my speculation).

In e/o (4), the majority of respondents may have considered that translating the words 'oil people' by 'compagnies pétrolières' ('oil companies') was legitimate and actually added value to the speech by making it more explicit and by using a word that the speaker may have been unable to retrieve due to lexical restriction. Other assessors may have considered that interpreters have no right to take such decisions (my speculation).

In e/o (5), in which 'countries' was translated by 'ceux' ('those people who'), the situation is opposite, with a loss of accuracy in the interpreter's speech. While some respondents may have missed the e/o, others may have considered that the loss was not significant (my speculation).

(4)   One further e/o not discussed above is an addition by the interpreter at the end of the speech extract, in the last sentence. He explains in French that the speaker is playing on the meaning of 'Rig' in the context of oil. This comment is clearly norm-based: the interpreter feels that it is appropriate to explain something that French speakers would miss otherwise. A few assessors only reported this as an e/o, probably meaning that some agreed with the norm, and some did not.

This last explicitation illustrates a point made earlier: the interpreter was able to abide by the norm and explain the use of 'rig' — which was later considered an error by some assessors — precisely because he was in control of the situation. Had he been under strong cognitive pressure due to high delivery speed or pressure from other input factors, he would have had to forego the explanation, and would have fared better in terms of propositional matching of source and target speech.

References

Barik, H. (1969) *A Study of Simultaneous Interpretation*. Unpublished doctoral dissertation, University of North Carolina.
Dodds, J. (1997) Introduction to the workshop report on the interaction between research and training. In Y. Gambier *et al.* (eds) *Conference Interpreting: Current Trends in Research* (pp. 89–92). Amsterdam and Philadelphia: Benjamins.
Gambier, Y., Gile, D. and Taylor, C. (eds) (1997) *Conference Interpreting: Current Trends in Research*. Amsterdam and Philadelphia: Benjamins.
Gardner, H. (1985) *The Mind's New Science*. New York: Basic Books.
Gerver, D. (1976) Empirical studies of simultaneous interpretation: A review and a model. In R. Brislin (ed.) *Translation: Application and Research* (pp. 165–207). New York: Gardner Press.
Gile, D. (1995a) *Basic Concepts and Models for Interpreter and Translator Training*. Amsterdam and Philadelphia: Benjamins.
Gile, D. (1995b) Fidelity assessment in consecutive interpreting: An experiment. *Target 7*, 151–64.
Gile, D. (forthcoming) Variability in fidelity perception.
The IR(TI)N Bulletin, issues 1–17, Paris.
Jones, R. (1997) *Conference Interpreting Explained*. Manchester: St Jerome.
Kopczynski, A. (1994) Quality in conference interpreting: Some pragmatic problems. In S. Lambert and B. Moser-Mercer (eds) *Bridging the Gap: Empirical Research in Simultaneous Interpretation* (pp. 87–99). Amsterdam and Philadelphia: Benjamins.
Kurz, I. (1996) *Simultandolmetschen als Gegenstand der Interdisziplinären Forschung*. Wien: WUV — Universitätsverlag.
Lambert, S. (1994) Foreword. In S. Lambert and B. Moser-Mercer (eds) *Bridging the Gap: Empirical Research in Simultaneous Interpretation* (pp. 5–14). Amsterdam and Philadelphia: Benjamins.
Lambert, S. and Moser-Mercer, B. (eds) (1994) *Bridging the Gap: Empirical Research in Simultaneous Interpretation*. Amsterdam and Philadelphia: Benjamins.
Morris, R. (1993) *Images of the Interpreter: A Study of Language-Switching in the Legal Process*. (Unpubished doctoral dissertation). Lancaster University.

Moser, P. (1997) Expectations of users of conference interpretation. *Interpreting* 1, 145–78.

Moser-Mercer, B. (1998) Measuring quality in interpreting. In *Evaluating an Interpreter's Performance* (pp. 39–47). University of Lodz: Centre for Modern Translation Studies.

Shlesinger, M. (1989) Extending the theory of translation to interpretation: Norms as a case in point. *Target* 1, 111–15.

Target 7 (1) (1995) Special issue on Interpreting Research.

Tommola, J. and Laakso, T. (1997) Source text segmentation, speech rate and language direction: Effects on trainee simultaneous interpreting. In K. Klaudy and J. Kohn (eds) *Transferre Necesse Est. Proceedings of the 2nd International Conference on Current Trends in Studies of Translation and Interpreting, 5–7 September, 1996, Budapest, Hungary* (pp. 186–91). Budapest: Scholastica.

Toury, G. (1995) *Descriptive Translation Studies and Beyond*. Amsterdam and Philadelphia: Benjamins.

Okay, So How Are Translation Norms Negotiated? A Question for Gideon Toury and Theo Hermans

Anthony Pym
Universitat Rovira i Virgili, Plaça Imperial Tàrraco 1, 43005 Tarragona, Spain

Norm, you see, was a typical Australian slob who watched football on television as he drank beer. Norm was the norm, or at least the behaviour pattern that the enlightened Australian government of the day was seeking to change. 'Life, be in it …', read the slogan that followed the image of Norm, telling us all to get up and do things. So the advertising campaign was aimed at changing a norm (changing, not necessarily breaking) and would seem to have been successful, to judge by the figures one now sees jogging along Australian beaches, not to mention the guilt I feel as I sit and watch football on television. One set of norms was transformed into another. And yet the change was by no means between equal objects; it required investment, effort, and exchange between people.

Now, norms are all very well. They exist, they change, and they can be changed from above or below, by reason, technology, or creativity. Norms are certainly part of anything we do, including translation. Their empirical study usefully insists that most of what we do, including translation, varies from place to place, time to time, and is subject to social conditioning. This relativist reminder is sometimes much needed. Yet the general concept of norms doesn't really get me moist in the nether regions, neither with excitement nor disgust. Why? Probably because norms, such as we find them in the papers by Gideon Toury and Theo Hermans, aren't really opposed to much except norms. You can have Norm 1 or Norm 2, or Norm 1.5 if necessary, as the scientific stance holds its object at arm's length to make the appropriate measurements. But what I don't find, or don't find enough of in the oppositions of norm and norm, is a radically opposed category that might broach what the Australian advertising campaign was all about: Is life, in any mildly participative sense, really just another set of norms? It could be more like the activity, the interactions, from which norms ensue and which they in turn constrain. No, I don't want to give a theory of life here. God forbid! What I want to do is simply to edge the descriptivists a little further out of their armchairs; I'd like them to participate in the active construction of their object, or, better, to recognise more consistently that this is what we are all doing.

My brief comments will thus focus on a question that remains largely unanswered in the papers by Toury and Hermans (nor really answered in the other material at hand, for example, Simeoni, 1998; Chesterman, 1997; Hermans, forthcoming). I want to ask about how norms might be related to some kind of participative social life. But I'll be more technical and ask how they are apparently 'negotiated' (since Toury uses the term). I would like to know how this is done, where it is done, and by whom.

Signs of Life?

The papers by Toury and Hermans both show signs of an aging structuralist empiricism (which they wouldn't name that way) adjusting to critical theory with a sociological bent (which they might indeed name that way).

In Toury, the signs of the adjustment are the relative absence of terms like 'system' or 'polysystem', and the robust presence of items like 'power relations', 'creativity', and 'social groups', as well as vague human things like 'hunches' and 'feelings'. I suspect all these newish elements could be aligned around the active verb 'to negotiate' ('norms are negotiated', etc.), since the term presupposes active human agents who are scarce, to say the least, in previous texts by Toury. Compare his paper in this volume with, for example, the second chapter of *Descriptive Translation Studies and Beyond* (1995), where norms are simply dropped in as an object to be studied on the basis of observed regularities of behaviour. There were no people doing anything in that chapter. Now, at least we have people 'negotiating', and thus, perhaps, we have some kind of social logic behind the emergence of norms.

Yet the adjustment is not quite as smooth as one might have hoped. Here we still find insistence on norms as behavioural 'regularities', as something that might be accessible to sociological statistics and fingers that can count (not that, to my knowledge, Toury has ever indulged in actual numbers — sociology is much easier to cite than to do). Here (in both Toury and Hermans) we still find that norms are meaningful in terms of the non-selection of available alternatives, which is about all that non-statistical structuralism ever had to say. And here (now specifically in Toury) we still find very positive values attached to the concepts of 'order' and 'predictability', apparently by a mind that very much wants our societies to make sense, to establish regularities, and to produce norms of one kind or another.

In Toury, the adjustment is helped by the recruitment of Davis and his explicit association of 'sociability' or 'social creativity' with 'order and predictability'. Other authorities could have supported similar associations (digging deeper, one might eventually reach the vitalist thought of Guyau's sociology, where 'sociability' was also the prime value). When people conform and work together, they are socially creative, and this is a good thing. Of course, Toury doesn't actually say 'this is a good thing', but I believe the implicatures are there. And the underlying thought is noble enough not to be taken as an insult. My only problem is that I, like many others of my generation, started theorising these things in the context of recycled *Tel Quel* revolutions, where absolute creativity ('productivité sans produit', said Kristeva at the time) required that all norms (usually in the guise of 'codes') be seen as ideological impositions, power-based constraints. They unacceptably restricted activities that were somehow opposed to norms: fractured subjectivities, subversive polysemy, the dynamics of difference, and associated battle-cries that you might remember if you were there at the time. From that perspective, you see, social life is not simply a matter of one norm against another, or of meaning ensuing from the selection of A rather than B, or of people politely socialising in order to agree on acceptable behaviour, or of analysts passively observing regular patterns. Much else was happening; even more was supposed to happen; and critical theory, by no means neutral, was supposed to help make it happen. Of course, we are no longer there ('violence' was a positive word then; now our politically correct radicals use it negatively). But some of us might quietly regret that, opposed to norms, we had, at the time, the seething dynamics of what I would now like to call, in memory of Guyau and the Australian government, 'life'. And that is precisely what I miss in Toury's somewhat forced compatibility of sociability and regularity. Without adequate attention to all those vital processes, the verb 'to negotiate', along with its refreshing companions, seems to be dangling on a loose end.

Theo Hermans would appear to have made the same adjustment in a rather more abrupt way. The careful, level-headed and cautious empiricist of the seminal *Manipulation* volume (1985) has somehow been seduced into full-blown critical theory of an even more postmodern ilk. I mean, we cruise along quite nicely with the story of the Flemish translator of Boethius; we are doing some kind of history or using concepts to investigate facts; and then, splash, we dive into the deep end of a strange theoretical certitude: 'Translations compound and intensify the refractory increase in voices, perspectives and meanings, they simultaneously displace and transform texts, and produce ...', and I spare you the rest. What is this? Certainly not a series of hypotheses awaiting falsification. I suspect that the sentence, and the five or so pages that follow it, is a report on theories read rather than translations studied. And since it has little to do with norms — they are not mentioned — let me summarily dispense with the matter: Sorry, but the vast majority of translations I deal with, even the ones I do, are linguistically and ideologically conservative because they reinforce imaginary boundaries between languages. Sorry, but the theoretical sleight of hand here is to attribute active verbs to translations as things (can objects really 'compound and intensify', 'displace and transform'?) rather than to translators as people (since I suppose that only subjects, be they producing or receiving, can properly 'negotiate'). Sorry, but I preferred the doubting Theo Hermans who once wanted to check such things.

Next question.

Where Do Norms Operate?

The signs of life are good. They are a generally positive development. Yet they tend to overshadow the specific question of norms in such a way that I'm no longer sure exactly where the norms are supposed to do their stuff. Consider Toury: 'whenever regularities are observed, they themselves are not norms [...], observed regularities testify to recurrent underlying motives'. So norms are somewhere behind or 'under' the regularities observed. Okay. Norms are also, apparently, the 'translation of general values or ideas shared by a community' (Toury, 1995: 55). So, if we can overlook the ineptitude of using the term 'translation' in a definition of translational phenomena, we have some kind of order or genealogy linking observed regularities, norms, and 'shared values', with the latter at the bottom of the heap. This is confusing because 'underlying motives' are not necessarily the same things as 'shared values'. It is also difficult to grasp because norms occasionally re-appear well beyond this eminently social embedding, as when Toury describes them as 'explanatory hypotheses', as something that the researcher ultimately invents in order to link observed regularities to some assumed 'underlying motives' or 'shared values'. Norms are thus at once somehow in the object and in the explanatory narrative. The trick, I suppose, is to ensure they're in both places at once, so that the ones we describe have as close a relation as possible to the ones we presume are there. But I'm not sure that Toury or Hermans really tell me how to do that. Because I'm not really sure where the 'there' is.

Let's take something that looks like a norm. John Milton (1994, 1996) has found that in a corpus of Brazilian translations of popular novels in the period 1943–1976, non-standard English is never rendered as non-standard Portuguese. Milton observes a regularity; he can construe at least one alternative to this regularity (i.e. translate into Brazilian dialects); he would thus appear to have bagged a norm. What is the norm? Apparently, to produce a 'more homogenised register than the sources', which Milton (1994: 28) actually calls a 'primary norm', with reference to Toury. But what is the difference between this 'norm' and the 'observed regularity'? Not much. The regularity supports the description, and the terms of the description are what looked for the regularity. This is because we have done nothing more than quantify one isolated variable. That doesn't get us very far until we start to tie that variable to a few other variables. I mean, the norm is fine, and might as well be identified with the observed regularity, but it has nothing much to say until correlated with something else. In an early paper, Milton does indeed find that the norm is associated with the presence of censorship, the officialist ideologies of the publishing houses concerned, the Brazilian military regime at the time, and the false image of a homogeneous and non-contestational society that must ensue from novels where everyone uses the same register. String all those variables together and we get something more than a banal regularity. We have started to explain how and why the norm might have come about; we have delved into the life behind the numbers; and we are using some kind of model to do so (in this case a dash of Althusser and Ideological State Apparatuses). Yet none of this can be definitive: in later papers Milton explains the same norm in terms of translators' rates of pay (they had no time to delve into dialect). In still more recent reflections (well, we were talking about it in the car this morning), Milton makes more of the fact that many of these novels were translated for children and adolescents, a sector in which the norm, for both translational and non-translational writing, was to use standard language only. So perhaps the translation norm was merely conforming to target-culture norms, in which case it would not really be a translation norm, would it?

I imagine Toury correcting me politely: No, he says, the norm is to conform, and I (and John Milton) have made the mistake of identifying the norm with the thing conformed to (the observed regularity). All right. It suits me quite well to locate properly translational norms in the space where one decides to accept or change target-culture norms, since that space is quite likely to be intercultural. But none of that terminological shuffling really solves the basic methodological problem. If the one dependent variable (refusal of non-standard language) can be explained in terms of variables involving political ideologies, translators' pay and norms for educational literature, to name but three possible paths, how are we to choose between these independent variables? How are we to interrelate them to form some kind of model?

Can Toury and Hermans help us with this problem? Can they tell us how variables might be strung together? And where, exactly, was the negotiating in this case? (Where, for that matter, was the 'refractory increase in voices'?)

If we really want to know where norms operate, I think we need to know more about what to do with terms like 'motives' and 'shared values' in contexts like this. The mere observation and description of norms doesn't explain a great deal. It just tells us that there are norms. We have to know about the other variables.

Who Negotiates Norms?

If there is to be negotiation, we need people able to negotiate. Who are these people? Where are they? Are they professionals, working on behalf of interested parties? Are they the principles themselves? Are they in the centres of cultures? Or perhaps in small groups along the edges?

In *Descriptive Translation Studies and Beyond*, Toury starts from a basic spatial binarism, assuming that translation 'involves at least two languages and two cultural traditions, i.e., at least two sets of norm-systems on each level' (Toury, 1995: 56). This seems to mean that norms are either on one side or the other, a division that does indeed underlie the 'initial norms' that involve adequacy or acceptability as a strategic aim. This sort of vision made life difficult for people, like myself, who think they find norms in the intersections or overlaps of cultures, in the intercultures where I suspect a lot of translators work. It also complicated things for people, like me, who suspect that norms found only on one side or the other are mostly not properly translation norms, since they tend to concern non-translational text practices as well as translation (e.g. standard language in educational books). Happily, when Toury addresses these questions now, he basically says all previous bets are off. Anything is possible. In each case you have to look around and see who and what the pertinent groups are. This is a huge advance on the previous binary thinking. Now we simply don't know.

How should we find out? Let me risk a practical suggestion. When deciding who the pertinent groups are, or indeed what independent variables are likely to be of interest, we should try to make sure the signs are there, somewhere in the documental object, and somehow related to a debate. This means reading the prefaces, the critical reactions, readers' responses, anything that can help locate arguments for or against the observed norm. This is more or less what Hermans does in his reading of de Buck. Catholic Flanders is not opposed to Protestant Holland simply because Hermans thinks this is the major division of the world (although Hermans does come from one side rather than the other); it is the division named in de Buck's preface. In Milton's study of popular novels, prefaces are used for similar orientation, although there, in a context of censorship, it is as important to read what was actively unsaid. If those signs were not there, researchers could more or less pick on any social group or banal regularity they liked, accumulating arbitrary variables in accordance with their latest readings in critical sociology. If the signs are there, and if they allow us to hypothesise that someone is arguing with someone else, it is usually not too difficult to dig around a little to locate those figures within quite specific social groups, which may or may not be within the one culture. Examples: In my work on Hispanic translation history, some of the debates are between the church and foreign translators (twelfth century), the church and the crown (transition to the thirteenth), the crown and Jewish translators (thirteenth), militant religious orders and Jewish translators (early fifteenth), a Spanish reformer and an Italian humanist (mid fifteenth), exiles and non-exiles (eighteenth to twentieth), reformists and aesthetes (twentieth), and so on. The groups are uneven in size, power, and cultural location. To that extent, Toury is quite right to leave the question as open as possible; he is correct to accept a far more fragmented social model than the systems to which he previously subscribed. But the centre of our interest, you see, has now shifted from the nature of the norms themselves to the social confrontations in which they are, indeed, negotiated.

Now, let me further suggest that, if such signs of debate can be located, there is no need to pay undue attention to many statistical regularities. When trying to locate a norm of some kind it is often enough to pick up traces of dissent or debate, or some degree of challenge to the norm. It is often of remarkably little consequence exactly what quantitative regularity is attached to the practices concerned; factors like authority or association with a dominant social group tend to be of rather more weight.

Several interesting things happen when we approach translation history in this way. Instead of compiling chronicles of stability (since that's what we first find when we start looking for norms), we approach the history of change (which is, after all, what history is all about). Instead of risking an arbitrary selection of regularities or social groups, we can at least point to evidence that might help tie our descriptions to things actually at work within the historical objects. And instead of mapping norms onto just one social group or dominant ideology, we start to see them as the results of disagreements bridged by adaptation and compromise.

If you like, John Milton would not really have to choose between variables concerning translators, political ideologies or literary genres. He might, for example, look for signs that an intercultural group of translators wanted to render all features of their source texts, that a group of nationalist educationalists sought to exclude translations altogether from the available children's literature, and that some kind of negotiation between the two resulted in translations being accepted without non-standard language. That is only a suggestion, a possible model. But it makes as much sense as norms that simply hang in the space of regularities, or norms that by definition belong on one side or the other.

Why I Prefer Negotiation

I do not pretend to have solved all the problems. And I'm not really here to sell my own replacements for norms. But I would like to stress, in semi-conclusion, some of the advantages that ensue from taking the term 'negotiation' seriously. I am aware that the term is often used as a conveniently vague metaphor, and that's how I suspect it is operating in Toury. And it must indeed be a metaphor in most of our studies. Translators, patrons and social groups very rarely actually come together to work out the norms that might enable them to work together despite their differences; we mostly have to see our field as if people were doing this, *as if* they were in a negotiation process. But the theories of that process can help us in several ways.

First, norms are already present in neo-classical negotiation theory (along with technical definitions of principles, rules, procedures, strategies and so on, offering us some quite precise analytical tools). Second, negotiation theorists are very much aware that norms are both part of what is to be agreed and part of the process of agreement (the most important norms are the ones that concern how the norms are to be negotiated). This imbrication may help us to think about the relations between the intercultural *how* of translation (properly translational norms, for me) and the *what* of the outcomes of translation (often the non-translational norms of target-culture genres). Third, negotiation theory generally sees the aim of these processes as being to facilitate cooperation despite difference, as opposed to the blunt differences that are now the gold sought by many of our relativist approaches. And fourth, neo-functionalist theories are starting to see how international institutions can become something more than the intergovernmental negotiations on which they are based, and how the agents can thus form epistemic communities that then oppose and overrule the principles that were originally represented (the European Court, for example, can oppose its member states). It could pay to ask if translators and their institutions might be able to function in such a way, at a level beyond the constitution of source and target cultures.

But to ask those questions, we have to think well beyond the level of culture-specific norms. Our attention should perhaps be focused on the human negotiators, the people involved in the development of translational norms, rather than on the mere apparition of the norms themselves. The papers by Toury and Hermans, in pointing to modes of life in and around norms, do much to initiate this process. But there is still a long way to go.

Life?

The Australian advertising campaign did much to change Norm's quotidian slobbery. How was this achieved? Basically, by producing a schematised representation of the norm to be changed. That is, by describing a particular set of norms. From this we might usefully learn that our descriptions of norms — be they those of Descriptive Translation Studies or of some kind of more critical theory — are far from neutral. When we describe, we immediately participate. This means that, as various social groups negotiate the norms of translation, we are not merely observers on the sidelines. It is good and pleasing to see Toury and Hermans loosening their lab coats a little and admitting, between the lines, to degrees of involvement. Whether we like it or not, some kind of life is at work in the negotiation of norms. And we are all in it.

References

Chesterman, A. (1997) *Memes of Translation*. Amsterdam and Philadelphia: Benjamins.
Herman, T. (forthcoming) *Translation in Systems. Descriptive and Systematic Approaches Explained*. Manchester: St Jerome.
Milton, J. (1994) A tradução de romances 'clássicos' do inglês para o português no Brasil. *Trabalhos em lingüística aplicada* 24, 19–33.
Milton, J. (1996) The translations of O Clube do Livro. *TradTerm* 3, 47–65.
Simeoni, D. (1998) The pivotal status of the translator's habitus. *Target* 10, 1–39.
Toury, G. (1995) *Descriptive Translation Studies and Beyond*. Amsterdam and Philadelphia: Benjamins.

Looking Through Translation: A Response to Gideon Toury and Theo Hermans

Douglas Robinson
Department of English, University of Mississippi, MS 38677, USA

These two essays by prime movers in what is variously called (by Toury) Descriptive Translation Studies (DTS) or (by Hermans) the Manipulation School, or, earlier (by Itamar Even-Zohar), polysystems theory, both focus on the impact on translation of social norms. Somewhat tongue-in-cheek, Toury traces the history of the study of norms in translation studies, not (quite) wanting to take full credit for the pioneering of this approach in the middle 1970s; certainly the study of translation norms has never been more current and vibrant than it is today, almost 25 years later, and much of the credit for *that* fact must surely be laid at Toury's feet.

The papers are very different. Toury's, outwardly the chattier and more casual of the two, is in fact the more tightly structured; in fact it offers an almost perfectly formed introduction to norms research as it is imagined in DTS. Hermans' piece, more formal in tone, is something of a grab-bag of different loosely fitting items: a brief history of a single translation, Adrianus de Buck's 1653 Dutch translation of Boethius's *Consolation of Philosophy*, in which he attempts to demonstrate in actual historiographical practise how translation norms are derived and how they must have worked; some broader theoretical frameworks for the study of social norms, borrowed from Niklas Luhmann and Pierre Bourdieu (both Toury and Hermans have found Daniel Simeoni's reading of Bourdieu exciting and productive for translation studies); some ruminations on what translation can teach us about culture; yet another attack on the notion of equivalence, even as hollowed out by Toury; some interesting but unfortunately truncated suggestions toward the theorisation of the 'translator function', based on earlier similarly truncated suggestions from Myriam Díaz-Diocaretz, Rosemary Arrojo, and me; and some concluding warnings against too scientific an approach to translation, based on the awareness that everything we say about translation is itself based on 'translations' or interpretations of texts.

For my purposes as respondent, Hermans' essay is the more interesting of the two; its looser structure, along with Hermans' willingness to get down and dirty with the practical processes of actually *doing* norm-governed translation history, gives me much more to say in a relatively short space than Toury's more theoretical piece.[1] What I propose to do, then, is to direct most of my remarks in the text to Hermans, and offer a few passing critiques of Toury in the endnotes.

Translation and Light

I want to begin my reading of Hermans' essay at what may seem at first a rather strange place. I want to approach it tropologically, eliciting from his metaphors for translation a cluster of images that will, I hope, suggest some important perspectives on the epistemological and hence also methodological problems that I see dogging the various descriptive approaches represented by these two essays.

Specifically, I want to read Hermans' essay first in terms of his metaphors of translation in terms of the passage through them of light: transparency and opacity. Here for example are two separate passages in Hermans' essay 'reflecting' (or refracting) the trope of the translation as either transparent or opaque:

> If translations were neutral, transparent, unproblematical, they would be dull and uninformative, either in themselves or as documents of cultural history and the history of ideas. They would be about as interesting as xerox machines. But because they are opaque, complicitous, and compromised, the history of translation supplies us with a highly charged, revealing series of cultural history and the history of ideas.

> ... in translating other people's concepts of translation ... our concepts are unlikely to hold up a transparent image. They must be based on concepts of translation. As we saw, precisely because translation is norm-governed and impregnated with values, it is never diaphanous, never innocent or transparent or pure, never without its own intermingled voices. On the contrary, it appropriates, transforms, deflects, and dislocates everything within its grasp.

The Greek and Latin words for substances that allow light to pass through them undistorted, 'diaphanous' and 'transparent', are associated here with neutrality, the absence of problems, dullness, a failure to inform; and, in the second passage, with innocence and purity. This would be, according to Hermans (and I would agree), more or less the traditional conception of translation in terms of equivalence. The opposite of transparency includes, in these two passages, opacity, complicity, compromise, high charge, revelation; and, in the second passage, impregnation with values, intermingled voices, appropriation, transformation, deflection, and dislocation. This latter list would cover his conception of translation as viewed through the norms concept.[2]

What leaps out at me immediately from those lists is the word *opacity*. Are translations really 'opaque'? What would that mean? 'Opaque' is obviously the polar opposite to 'transparent', so if Hermans is trying to convince us that his norms approach to translation is radically different from the traditional approach that he associates with transparency, without a doubt opacity is the image to use. But what does it *mean*? Lawrence Venuti uses it, too, in his introduction to *Rethinking Translation*, where he encourages us (and more specifically the translator) to treat words as material things, i.e., to respect 'their opacity, their resistance to empathic response and interpretive mastery' (1992: 4). So Hermans is not alone in his use of this imagery. But I still don't understand it. How are words ever material or opaque? What would an opaque translation be? One you can't see through, obviously; but what would the trope of 'seeing through' signify here?

What, for that matter, does the transparency of a translation mean? Hermans speaks of 'hold[ing] up a transparent image', which sounds almost like an oxymoron to me: an image you can see through. See through to what? I assume he means by transparency something like the traditional notion that the translation should be a window to the original: a piece of glass held up between the viewer and the original, so as to make it fully and undistortedly visible. Elsewhere he writes, summarising this traditional view: 'A translation most coincides with its original when it is most transparent, when it approximates pure resemblance'. This offers two different metaphors for translation, clearly (an adverb Hermans is fond of, and why not, as it fits the general transparency trope quite nicely — more of that below), one of the window, the other of the copy. The copy presumably would be opaque too, but since those two images belong to two different metaphorical fields, it would be unfair to stress that (unless the transparency of the *image* is a blending of the two fields?). The transparency or opacity of a translation hinges on our (in)ability to see through it to the original; the resemblance between a copy and an original depends on our ability to look back and forth between them and make comparisons.

A focus on transparency and opacity, then, suggests that Hermans is troping norm-governed translation in terms of its ability to *block* our vision of the original. This seems strange, but what else could opacity mean? The other words he uses to describe translation in a norms approach do not suggest this blocking, so we might want to give him the benefit of the doubt and suggest that he does not really *mean* opacity, even figuratively, let alone literally. What he really means, say, is translucence, or some other form of visual distortion, the creation of a distortive or corrective (or, more neutrally, 'transformative') lens of some sort. Certainly his vocabulary for the norm-governed conception of translation that he prefers includes eulogistic images of 'seeing through', especially of revelation, which is to say of tearing away the veil ('the history of translation supplies us with a highly charged, *revealing* series of cultural history'), and of deflection ('it appropriates, transforms, deflects, and dislocates everything within its grasp') — which in an optical imagery might better be called *refraction*. Most of his eulogistic words, in fact, suggest the distortion of vision, not its total blockage. But he keeps repeating that the translation is specifically *opaque*: 'First, what makes translation interesting as a cultural phenomenon is precisely its lack of transparency, i.e. its opacity and complicity … Translation is necessarily hybrid, overdetermined, opaque, different'. This puzzles me. Yes, translations deflect, refract, distort the 'light' by which we see the original. But what do we gain by imagining them as *blocking* that light? Should we be imagining the translator as deliberately or inevitably alienating the target reader from the source text or author or culture, making the source text inaccessible to the target reader? Or what?

Epistemology as 'Seeing Through'

The epistemological problem that this light imagery can point us to, I suggest, revolves around the implications of 'clarity', a word which in its adverbial form runs like a scarlet thread all through Hermans' essay:

De Buck's selection is *clearly* governed by and in turn strengthens already strong normative constraints.

In other words, through de Buck's comments the boundaries of translation as he and presumably a number of his contemporaries understand them, come *clearly* into view as well. (Emphasis in both cases added)

And so on. Just what kind of clarity are we talking about here? I think we can 'clearly' see that it has something to do with seeing; perhaps more specifically with *seeing through*. There is something to be seen; it needs to be seen clearly. What we need is a lens for seeing it clearly. I'm not sure 'clearly' and 'transparently' are synonymous here, but 'clearly' they are closely related. Hermans wants us to be able to see something without distortion, which was more or less the express goal of translation conceived as 'transparent' as well.

The issue is considerably more complicated than I am making it seem so far, of course; I am just trying to get the key images out on the table. At first blush it does seem, however, as if Hermans wants a kind of clarity out of translation studies that he does not want (or does not think it possible to obtain) out of translation. Certainly there is a conceptual conflict in his insistence that the history of opaque translation 'supplies us with a highly charged, revealing series of cultural history and the history of ideas'. If translation is opaque, what can it reveal? If translation is opaque, surely it is the veil that must be *removed* before it can reveal anything? But this is 'clearly' not what Hermans wants to say. He wants to say, I think, that we can see cultural history and the history of ideas *through* translation. Clearly. Without distortion? Perhaps not; Hermans is much more aware of the epistemological complexities involved here than, say, Toury (see especially Hermans' concluding section, 'Translating Translation'). But perhaps with minimal distortion.

> Translation is opaque.
> Translation is a distorting lens that we see through only with difficulty.
> Translation can reveal cultural history clearly.

Three significantly different epistemologies, 'clearly'. And all of them are operant, though perhaps only subliminally, imagistically, rhetorically, in this one essay.

What this epistemological morass means for Hermans is a good deal of methodological slipping and sliding. For example, in his illustration of the importance of norms in translation history, the story of de Buck's Dutch translation of Boethius's *Consolation of Philosophy*, it is never quite 'clear' what sort of method he is applying. All we know is that it is wrapped up with the discovery or inference of 'norms' that (must have) constrained de Buck's work. Hermans defines his method as follows: 'Since a norms-based approach to translation starts from the assumption that the translation process involves decision-making on the part of the translator, it will focus on the question of what choices are made in relation to available alternatives, and what it is that steers translators towards one preferred option rather than another'. The word 'focus' suggests here that the 'object' to be seen 'clearly' would be the translator's specific 'choices', or decision-making process. This of course is a psychological black box that the think-aloud protocols people have been trying to solve in the present, with living subjects and tape recorders, but with massive epistemological problems nonetheless (how can we ever *know* that what the subjects say corresponds to what they are actually thinking or doing in their heads as they translate?). With long-dead translators from three and a half centuries ago, the epistemological problems proliferate. How can we ever hope to know what de Buck was thinking in translating this way or that?

Well, we have his translation, of course. We know some of the political and social history of the Low Countries in the mid-seventeenth century (and Hermans reviews that briefly for us). That's about it. Some words on the page, purporting to be de Buck's translation of Boethius; some words on other pages, purporting to be what really happened in the Low Countries three and a half centuries ago. From these textual materials, Hermans proposes to elicit de Buck's translatorial decision-making process — to get inside the translator's head. Descriptively. And clearly.

A tall order. The main problem Hermans faces, of course, is that texts tell us precious little about their authors, and what little they do tell, they do not tell clearly. Hermans wants de Buck's translation to hold up a transparent image to de Buck's translatorial choices, but he has just been telling us that translations do not hold up transparent images, so he is in a bit of a quandary.

His solution is to argue circularly. He does not explicitly call this a hermeneutical circle, but since that is the most generous reading I can place on his argumentative style, I will assume that that is how he intends it to be read. For example:

> Why Boethius? Just as Boethius drew comfort from philosophical speculation at a time when he was in prison awaiting execution, so the hard-pressed citizens of Flanders will derive consolation from reading Boethius in their hour of need. That is what makes Boethius an apt choice for de Buck. In preference to an unspecified number of alternative possibilities. Just how many possibilities were realistically available to de Buck is obviously impossible to ascertain. The list will almost certainly have included works such as Justus Lipsius' *De constantia* of 1584. Lipsius was a Catholic writer and enjoyed international fame as a Humanist at Louvain University, barely fifty miles from de Buck's town of Veurne. His *De constantia*, a dialogue in the Stoic tradition, had been written, like Boethius' *Consolation*, to find equanimity amid a sea of troubles and proved an immediate European bestseller.

And so on. De Buck chose Boethius because his Flemish compatriots needed consolation; and we know that because there were other Latin works offering consolation that de Buck could have chosen to translate instead. De Buck could have chosen another work offering consolation; hence his choice of Boethius had something to do with his desire to offer consolation. X, therefore Y; Y, therefore X. As Hermans himself puts it, in classically circular style: 'In other words, highlighting obvious but excluded alternatives allows us to appreciate the significance of de Buck's selection, as we can see him making his own choice optimally relevant in view of what is already available in terms of suitable source texts. In providing solace and a morale-booster his translation constitutes an answer to a perceived problem'. The alternative Hermans highlights is 'obvious' to him because he has already decided that de Buck wanted to offer the Flemish consolation: that's how he happens upon Lipsius. Once he has happened on Lipsius, the 'exclusion' of *De constantia* as a source text helps him see 'clearly' that de Buck's choice of Boethius really did have something to do with a desire to console the Flemish.

The last part of that is especially significant: 'his translation constitutes an answer to a perceived problem'. My question is, who 'perceives' the problem ('clearly')? Presumably, for Hermans, de Buck. Actually, of course, it is Hermans, as he himself freely admits later in his essay ('It is, as always, the observer who constructs the case before him or her, rendering data relevant by deploying them as evidence'). So 'his translation constitutes an answer to a perceived problem' could be read in at least two mutually contradictory ways, revolving around the identity of the perceiver and the interpretation we place on the polysemous word 'constitutes':

(a) De Buck's translation is an answer to the problem de Buck himself perceived (i.e. that Flanders needed consolation).
(b) Using de Buck's translation Hermans *creates* (generates, construes) an answer to the problem Hermans perceives (i.e. that Flanders in de Buck's day needed consolation).

In (a), the object is seen clearly, without the distorting lenses of historical interpretation (or the textual evidence that is thus interpreted). A problem exists. De Buck perceives it. By translating Boethius, he solves it, or at least offers a solution to it. In (b), the hermeneutical distortions of all interpretive lenses are everywhere present. Hermans has a text, and doesn't know what to do with it. He wants to say something about it. He wants to say something about norms in connection with it. But there are no norms 'clearly' visible in it. So he 'constitutes' them out of the translation, out of the text, by circular reasoning: this and that feature of the text suggests the operation of norms in society; the operation of those norms gave the text the shape it has. For example:

> The fact however that in both these cases he feels the need explicitly to justify his recourse to a paraphrastic mode with reference to specific places and specific reasons suggests that, although it is a legitimate form of translating and hence one that meets existing expectations about what constitutes translation, i.e. one that stays within the perimeter policed by the constitutive norms and conventions of translation, de Buck recognises it as more marginal than the 'standard' mode of translation. This is presumably because paraphrase, requiring the translator to speak more overtly in his or her own name, tends to forms such as glossing, commentary, or imitation. These forms are all adjacent to, may occasionally overlap with but are definitely not coterminous with the prevailing concept of translation. In other words, through de Buck's comments the boundaries of translation as he and presumably a number of his contemporaries understand them, come clearly into view.

The textual evidence Hermans is working from here is that de Buck tells his readers that he has translated the title of Boethius's book 'in an explanatory manner' (*tot breeder verklaringh*), and some of his translations of the more difficult poems are (literally) 'a little wide-loping' or (more paraphrastically) 'somewhat circumambulatory' (*een luttel wijdt-loopigh*). All the rest of that analysis of the norms and conventions and boundaries impinging on de Buck's work is built, by logical inference, out of those two brief phrases — well, those phrases and the knowledge, whose source we are not given, that paraphrase is not generally considered 'coterminous' with another approach to translation that Hermans calls 'standard' and 'prevailing'. Prevailing in de Buck's time and place? Presumably; but presuming seems to be all Hermans is doing as well. We have documented evidence (not in this essay, but for example in Robinson, 1997) of numerous remarks from other times and places in translation history suggesting that many people did not consider paraphrase 'true' translation, or the 'best' kind of translation; did that attitude 'prevail' in the mid-seventeenth-century Low Countries as well? We are not told; certainly if Hermans has historical evidence for this he doesn't give it to us. And his use of the present tense ('may occasionally overlap with but are definitely not coterminous with') suggests that he is in fact referring to an ahistorical or transhistorical conception of translation that he merely *presumes* would have prevailed in de Buck's society as well, because de Buck described two parts of his translation as 'explanatory' and 'circumambulatory', which sound roughly congruent with 'paraphrastical'.

And the result of all this circular presuming? We are handed two inferences about de Buck's specific norm-bound choices, now explicitly called 'facts': that he 'felt the need' to justify his approach explicitly, and that he 'recognises it as more marginal'. Based on these 'facts' Hermans is able to conclude: 'through de Buck's comments the boundaries of translation as he and presumably a number of his contemporaries understand them, come clearly into view'. I wouldn't call the textual evidence or the interpretive presumptions by which Hermans arrives at this presentation of his 'object' opaque, exactly; but they are not really what I would want to call 'clear' or 'transparent', either. Perhaps they are simply as distortive as the lenses that, he says, are found in all translation.

History, Science, and Hermeneutics

It may simply be bad timing that Hermans wrote this paper *before* Anthony Pym's horizon-expanding book *Method in Translation History* (1998) came out, and the paper was sent to me for comment *after* the book was out and I had read it. For in light of Pym's systematic and comprehensive methodological guide, Hermans' discussion of de Buck looks suspiciously like bad historiography. Pym leans more toward an empirical, positivistic, Popperian view of historiography than I do, and some of his book may be subject to intense criticism; but the book does suggest to me that descriptive historians of translation may need to do more than simply construe norms from the translations and paratexts that are supposedly constrained by them.[3] As Pym makes clear, part of the problem underlying norms research as it is practised today by DTSers like Toury and Hermans is that it aspires to the status of an empirical or objective or positive science, when norms (unlike, say, rocks) have no positive existence to be empirically described. They are really, as Toury seems almost-but-not-quite ready to admit in his own essay, just a way of *talking* about the feeling we have that our behaviour is guided by social constraints — subjective forces rather than objective ones, even if the subjectivity involved is by definition a collective one, or, perhaps, arises out of the dialectical interchange between individuals and collectives.[4] If the DTS scholars are to continue to present their findings as descriptive 'science', they need to focus far more attention on their methodologies (and perhaps that will be one of the results of Pym's book).

If we imagine DTS as qualitative empirical research, for example, we would expect researchers in the field to make some effort at triangulation — seeking corroborating evidence of translational norms from sources outside the translations and translation paratexts themselves, so as to offer *some* sort of substantiation for the 'explanatory hypotheses' that norms currently must remain. This sort of triangulation will not solve the epistemological problems raised by this sort of research, but it might mitigate the worst methodological effects of those problems somewhat.

Then again, such triangulation may simply prove impossible. After all, what other sources do exist for these norms but the textual ones that these scholars are already using? The qualitative DTSer cannot exactly engage in participant observation in the seventeenth century, or send de Buck a questionnaire. If this is the case — if norms research is never going to get more scientific than it is today — DTS scholars might want to consider formulating more hermeneutical methods based expressly on the close reading of texts and philosophical speculation, such as the one Friedrich Nietzsche developed in *A Genealogy of Morals*, or Sigmund Freud developed in *Civilization and its Discontents*, or Kenneth Burke developed in *The Rhetoric of Religion*, or (gentle reader) your humble author developed in *Translation and Taboo*. I am certainly not saying I want the DTS group to flock to my 'camp' (indeed if I found that I *had* a camp, I would immediately set about pulling up tent stakes and smothering the campfires with dirt). But hermeneutics at least has a philosophically sophisticated methodology that is well-suited to the materials it attempts to explain — and also, as I have been suggesting, to the elucidation of such nebulous forces as social norms. If in fact there is no way norms can be reliably evidenced, if all we have to work with in the descriptive exploration of norms and their impact on translations is speculative inferences from texts, then the hermeneutical circle would be a much more productive tool than the scientistic pretense that inference and idealisation can ever yield hard data — that the 'explanatory hypotheses' Toury calls norms can ever be empirically verified.

And if the only consideration that prevents the DTSers from making the leap into unabashed hermeneutics remains a pining for the institutional status and clout of 'science', they might as well give it up. Failed scientism, impossible scientism, only makes the greatest strengths of this approach — close textual exegesis, elaborate philosophical systems, imaginative speculation — look like its points of greatest weakness.

Notes

1. This is, in fact, somewhat ironic, given Toury's express preference for research over theory: 'As always, my main interest lies with *descriptive-explanatory* research rather than mere theorising. For me, theory formation within Translation Studies has never been an end in itself. Its object has always been to lay a sound basis and supply an elaborate frame of reference for controllable studies into actual behaviour and its results and the ultimate test of theory is its capacity to do that service'.
    Theory-formation may for Toury not be an end in itself, but in this essay the 'true' end of studying translational behaviour is certainly deferred. He offers a few very brief examples from translation history (cf. paragraph 4.10), and even there gives no indication of how norms should actually be derived from observed regularities.
2. The juxtaposition of 'impregnation' with 'innocence/purity' suggests that Hermans

is also working with a sexual metaphor for translation that I don't have the space to explore in detail here: the translation is a woman who is either pure and innocent, i.e. a virgin, or she has had sex and got pregnant. This metaphor runs all through the history of translation theory, especially in writers like Herder ('A language before all translations is like a maiden who has not yet lain with a foreigner and borne a child of mixed blood: for the time being she is still pure and innocent, a true image of the character of her people. She is also poor, obstinate, and unruly; and as she is, so is the original and national language' [Robinson, 1997: 208]) and Schleiermacher ('Who would willingly breed mongrels when he could instead sire loving children in the pure image of their father?' [Robinson 1997: 232]). Note that Hermans himself derides the traditional view of translation as 'sexist in casting translation in the role of maidservant, faithful and obedient wife, or "*belle infidèle*"'.

3. Here is Toury on this topic, from his essay: 'Needless to say, whatever regularities are observed, they themselves are not the norms. They are only external evidence of the latter's activity, from which the norms themselves (that is, the 'instructions' which yielded those regularities) are still to be extracted; whether by scholars wishing to get to the bottom of a norm-governed behaviour or by persons wishing to be accepted to the group and hence needing to undergo *socialisation* ...'

   Note the trope, which parallels Hermans' 'clarity' and 'transparency': 'scholars wishing to *get to the bottom*'. You dig down until you hit pay-dirt. At the bottom. Once you extract or excavate the norms from underneath the rubble of regularities on top of them, you see them clearly. The norms are there; they are simply hidden beneath the translations themselves. The idealised process behind norms research, then, is this: read the translation; observe the regularities; extract from those regularities the 'norms'; imagine those 'norms' governing the translator's translational behaviour and generating the regularities; act as if the norms preceded the imaginative process that constituted them.

4. Toury again: 'There is an interesting reversal of direction here: whereas in actual practice, it is subjugation to norms that breeds norm-governed behaviour which then results in regularities of surface realisations, the search for norms within any scholarly programme must proceed the other way around. Thus, it is regularities in the observable results of a particular kind of behaviour, assumed to have been governed by norms, which are first noted. Only then does one go on to extract the norms themselves, on the (not all that straightforward) assumption that observed regularities testify to recurrent underlying motives, and in a direct manner, at that. Norms thus emerge as *explanatory hypotheses* (or observed [results of] behaviour) rather than entities in their own right'.

   This is very close to my own hermeneutical critique of this methodology: Toury admits at the end of that passage that norms are explanatory fictions or hypotheses, not realities or 'entities in their own right'. At the beginning of the passage, however, he still wants to insist that the norms actually exist: 'in actual practice, it is subjugation to norms that breeds norm-governed behaviour which then results in regularities of surface realisations'. The norms really are there. They really do subjugate translators, govern their behaviour, and so cause regularities in translations for scholars to observe. DTS is still a *science*, which proceeds by reliable methods of observation and idealisation. The problem with this thematisation of the method, however, is that the hypotheses called 'norms' can never be verified or falsified. They remain hypotheses, which is to say, fictions.

References

Pym, A. (1998) *Method in Translation History.* Manchester: St. Jerome.
Robinson, D. (1997) *Western Translation Theory From Herodotus to Nietzsche.* Manchester: St. Jerome.
Venuti, L. (ed.) (1992) *Rethinking Translation.* London: Routledge.

The Limitations of the Strictly Socio-Historial Description of Norms: A Response to Theo Hermans and Gideon Toury

Sergio Viaggio
United Nations, Vienna International Centre, P.O. Box 500, 1400 Vienna, Austria

Introduction

I wish to take issue with the following crucial contention in Toury's thought provoking piece:

> For me, theory formation within Translation Studies has never been an end in itself. Its object has always been to lay a sound basis and supply an elaborate frame of reference for controllable studies in actual behaviour and its results and the ultimate test of theory is its capacity to do that service. (Paragraph 1)

Two pages later, he adds that:

> ... the difficulties I had stemmed from the very nature of the essentialistic definition, imposing as it does a deductive mode of reasoning, rather than the formulation of any single definition. Even the most flexible of these definitions, as long as it still purported to list the necessary and sufficient conditions for an entity to be regarded as translational, proved to be unworkable. (Paragraph 2)

Too bad, but for me, on the other hand, the ultimate object of theory is its capacity to account for all relevant phenomena. Translation Studies cannot stop at observing, registering and describing actual translational behaviour, at eliciting from it what often turns out to be mostly intuitive, semiconscious or even a-critical norms (valuable as the endeavour is). Rather, it must strive to differentiate within that mess of a mass *methodologically competent* behaviour, the kind of behaviour that impels actual progress by fostering scientifically progressive norms. This Translation Studies can only hope to achieve by becoming what so many thinkers dread: Translatology, a discipline based on its own domain-specific theory. Translation Theory has the following tasks: (a) to define the essence of translation, or, if you dread the term, its constitutive rules — what translation is, always, as opposed to any other communicational phenomena, in order in that light (b) to explain why it is that translations can be and indeed are different — that they can follow different norms and still qualify as translations; and (c) to help assess different methods, products and norms as more or less apt or efficient as a function of the task in hand. In other words, like other theories, translation theory must define the *essence* of its object of study, and only then proceed to explain and describe its actual *existence*, making apparent, as a consequence, ways for the development and improvement of both processes and products (whence its decisive didactical importance). Needless to say, as any social object translation will have fuzzy edges, imperceptibly 'degenerating' into non-translation. That too is to be accounted for by its theory.

The reason we are still debating such basic epistemological questions is due, I submit, to the extremely recent social recognition of translation as an economically significant activity, inextricably and dialectically linked to the development of the productive forces of society. This recognition has been both the consequence and the cause of a dramatic increase in the need for down-to-earth, nonce pragmatic translations, which has entailed the need to train translators and interpreters efficiently and in great numbers; whence, in turn, the tremendous development of academic research and scientifically based theoretical thinking. Nowadays, observing and describing translational behaviour in a theoretical vacuum makes as much sense as the sociohistorical observation and description of medical behaviour. If what interests us is not the history but the therapeutic potential of medicine, it is not enough behaviourally to describe how physicians go or have gone about treating specific patients or diseases: we must ask whether, given the knowledge and resources available at a given time and place, a specific instance of medical behaviour is/was *competent*, to what extent and why.

As Toury rightly points out, the weakness of descriptive translation studies is that it has focused almost exclusively on literary translation and norms: as literature itself, literary translation is remiss to objective assessment — if not with respect to obvious translation 'mistakes', then *vis-à-vis* translational methodology. On the other hand, if the evolution of nonliterary translation norms were addressed, I am certain that it would evince a remarkable parallelism to economic development, with the communicatively aptest norms gaining the upper hand in the most industrially advanced and educationally developed societies. Now that pragmatic translation is by far the main field of translational activity,[1] the one schools train students and business and international organisations hire translators for, the question is legitimately posed whether the strictly sociohistorical study of norms actually helps to (a) understand translation better, (b) translate better and, (c) teach to translate better. Is the sociohistorical study of what astronomers have thought about the heavens above relevant to our present understanding of the universe? Is Ptolemy scientifically relevant today? Is St Jerome? Or are there objective, knowable laws, principles and facts, neurophysiological, cultural, social and generally communicational that allow us to understand how different approaches actually work, regardless of the historically and culturally conditioned subjective intuitions of individual practitioners in different places at different times? If such objective criteria — or, if you prefer, knowledgeable inter-subjective agreement on objective facts — is impossible, then everything goes and there is nothing left for us to teach, or learn, or simply do better.

Except that, fortunately, there is: We can safely teach, for instance, that, whilst the aptness of the semantic vs communicative norms may remain moot in the exalted, largely subjective heights of literature, when it comes to efficient pragmatic communication, an unabashedly communicative translation — one that is clearer, shorter, more elegant, more user-friendly than its original — is not simply a token of a *different* norm: it is a token of a *better* norm. This widely shared view is not the result of a new 'cultural' norm come from without our discipline, but of our own deeper collective awareness of what translation is, is supposed to be and function as — an effective form of mediated interlingual intercultural communication. As we approach the third millennium, translational norms are finally ceasing to be simply a cultural-bound concept, and becoming based on an ever deeper knowledge of the objective laws governing communication through speech. The big difference between our present-day discussion and the debates before the explosion of scientific knowledge about human communication is akin to the difference between the arguments of ancient philosophers and modern-day scientists on, say, the nature of matter. Leucippus and Democritus could only guess that the universe is made up of minuscule particles — we know better: we know it for a fact. When it comes to translation as a form of mediated interlingual intercultural communication (an essence that had escaped every single translator until fairly recently), we do or at least should indeed know better — and make no apologies for it.

The Grounds for a General Theory of Translation

I submit that, by now, enough relevant factors entering into play in communication have been accounted for to allow any competent and industrious translator adequately to chart his or her course from any source text to a communicationally apt target text. Again, this is what a scientific theory of translation can and must help him achieve, allowing, at the same time, for the descriptive, normative and prescriptive nature of translatology to become harmoniously synthesised (as attempted by Chesterman, 1997). As Marx put it, science is but praxis made awareness. Now that the basic elements are conceptualised and translation has finally become the subject of systematic thought and research, and not merely an individual practice by isolated individuals, it is time for a new cycle to begin: a general theory of translation has not only become possible — it already exists. It is far from the end of the road, but a decisive stage has been reached.

What Translation Is

Translation is a subtype of interlingual, intercultural and mediated communication, that intervenes when the participants in the communicative event (co-present or centuries and oceans apart) require a mediator conversant with the different languages and cultures involved. This communicative essence of translation has been intuitively quite clear from the very beginning. The great contradictory insights, the constant oscillation between *sensum de senso* and *verbum e verbo*, the two Schleiermacherian directions, *les belles infidéles*, Savory's dichotomies, Newmark's semantic and communicative approaches, the tug-of-war between *sourcières* and *ciblistes*, etc. have been ever closer intuitive approximations of what precisely is to be communicated by the translator, and how. The basic question boils down to what communication is (in general, and, more specifically, mediated interlingual intercultural communication) and the conditions for its success. The answer, again, is only possible if we contemplate the phenomenon in its totality: As García Landa analyses in a private letter, communication is a historically conditioned social event — or rather a countless number of events — whereby human beings produce and exchange speech-informed second-degree perceptions. These exchanges are possible because evolution has produced socio-neuronal systems that allow us to apprehend, segment, conceive, imagine, analyse, store, retrieve and convey experience through the organising filter of a Pavlovian second signal-system, i.e. of signs with conventional referential value — signs not of 'things', but of our perceptions and representations. This is the basis for his (now our) General Theory of Translation.

A General Theory of Translation

So what is translation? What García Landa (1990, 1998) explains: a special way of speaking — speaking in order to re-say *'what has been said'* — or written or spoken through gestures;[2] re-producing in a new act of speech and in a different language what has been said in a previous act of speech[3] (which excludes both intralingual and inter-semiotic 'translation', close neighbours that they are). *'What has been said'*, i.e. meaning meant, sense: both readers or listeners of the original and addressees of a translation expect to understand it; all translators are bent on conveying it. Every single act of translation can be reduced to this bare essential — the immigrant kid 'naturally' or 'natively' interpreting for her mother at the social welfare office, the poor student struggling with a translation exercise, Nabokov obsessed with milking the last seme out of Pushkin's *Eugene Onegin*, Nida changing biblical kisses into handshakes, and the simultaneous interpreter struggling with accent, speed and bad sound are all involved in reproducing a perceptual space, a speech-informed perception verbalised in one language by means of a new formal space, a verbalisation in a different language. The subsidiary polemics revolves basically around different concepts of (a) the ontological and logical status of the specific linguistic signs *vis-à-vis* meaning meant; (b) the relative weight of relevance for the addressor(s) *vis-à-vis* relevance for the addressee(s) in the reproduction of the speech perception; and (c) the degree of free choice the translator has in his or her capacity as a mediator in either respect.

From a purely descriptive standpoint norms are but regular patterns of behaviour observed as people (naively or scientifically, awkwardly or adroitly) go about reproducing speech perceptions in a different language with the aim of having their addressees relevantly understand the original one.[4] Since neither linguistics nor, for that matter, literary studies can explain comprehension, they cannot explain communication or translation either. In order to come of age, translatology must wean itself both from the 'scientific' paradigm of linguistics, and from the 'humanistic' paradigm of philology. With all due deference to Toury and so many other outstanding scholars, anybody refusing to let go, I am afraid, is holding us back. The truly *scientific* way of going about translating, I insist, consists in applying the latest insights into speech production and comprehension (and all other relevant to communication, including, to be sure, literary and philological knowledge) in order to ensure maximum efficiency at defining and accomplishing the task specifically in hand — i.e. to insure optimally relevant identity between meaning meant and meaning understood.[5]

A corollary of the above is that a scientific theory of translation must also identify the conditions for such optimality in each specific case, or at least, in typical situations. I cannot explore this question any further here, but simply wish to stress what should be the overriding 'essentialistic' purpose of Translation Theory: no unified notion of its object — no object to describe.

The Chasm Between Professional and Expectancy Norms

Nowhere is this 'essentialistic' view of translation as necessary and apparent as in translator training. The social responsibility of translation teachers is to transform natural talent into professional ability, i.e. into *competent* professional practice. As evaluators and examinators, pedagogues assess their students' performance against their own quality standards: they decide what counts as quality and, therefore, competence. They are thus contributing to setting *professional norms* — the norms against which peers judge their own and their colleagues' performance. With the theoretical buttressing of the most competent practitioners, the divide between scientific and naive professional norms widens, which in turn tends to generate a chasm between the former and expectancy norms — the norms against which the layman assesses translators (see Chesterman, 1997 and Simeoni, 1998). The difference between translation and better established professions is that in the latter case expectancy norms have become based on professional norms rather than the other way around, so that no patient will question, for instance, the surgeon's 'right' to amputate, provided that he — and eventually his peers — think it is the best alternative under the circumstances — best for the task at hand, i.e. doing what is best for the patient. The reason for this abyss is sociohistorical: physicians, architects, engineers and other professionals have scientifically, practically and therefore socially established themselves as experts in their field; and in so doing have earned the trust of users of their services, who, at worst, are willing to give them the benefit of the doubt. This they have managed through centuries of actually striving to grasp more and more thoroughly the laws objectively governing relevant physical and social phenomena, and ever more effectively putting them to practical use. As a consequence, their scientific competence informs their professional performance thereby ensuring its validity. The most obvious social consequence thereof is that their diplomas are recognised and protected, and that, through their professional organisations, they have the right to regulate both access to the profession and professional practice.

Translators, on their part, have not yet collectively succeeded in theorising their praxis, and have yet to establish themselves and the profession to a similar extent, which makes them feel much more at the mercy of their users than other professionals. This is an objective vulnerability: Although recognised practitioners do normally have the linguistic and thematic competence necessary for effecting most 'meaning' (i.e. basically semantic) transfers adequately, many generally lack the theoretical competence to ensure and/or defend the communicative validity of their options. It is here, at the metalingual, communicative level — the mediator's highest instance — that the translator's right to 'tamper with' the original is posed. The question, then, is not whether but to what extent and in what circumstances the translator can *legitimately* or *advisedly* improve or fail to improve, adapt or fail to adapt his or her verbalisation of sense, i.e. without overstepping the deontological boundaries of loyalty. The answer, once again, cannot but be based on the best knowledge available about the social and physical rules objectively governing communication: Without such theoretical buttress, even the best intuitions fail to assert themselves procedurally, whereby professional norms remain naive. The main difference between scientific and naive professional norms, then, revolves around the translator's role, responsibility, freedom and loyalty as an *interlingual intercultural mediator*.

Yes, I am one of those teachers (*cum* practitioner *cum* administrator) that, as Toury puts it, 'see it as their task to effect changes in the world at large' (or, more modestly, in the way translation is thought of by scholars, practised by translators and valued by society), even if it is 'one which others, including the group of practising translators, may well regard as perfectly satisfactory' (paragraph 4.9). Sometimes science knows no other way of progressing — quite a few thinkers have paid for it with their very lives.

Correspondence

Any correspondence should be directed to Sergio Viaggio, United Nations, Vienna International Centre, P.O. Box 500, 1400 Vienna, Austria (sviaggio@unov.un.or.at).

Notes
1. Nowadays, with publishing turned into a big transnational business, many kinds of erstwhile literary translating can be considered pedestrianly pragmatic.
2. A general theory of translation cannot leave out sign languages and must account for translation both among and across oral and sign languages.
3. García Landa developed this theory in his unpublished doctoral dissertation. I found that his way of modelling a speech act and presenting translation as a second speech act sharing the same perceptual space is a powerful tool for understanding translating as a special mode of talking. On that basis, we think that we have succeeded in producing a powerful comprehensive theory of communication through speech that we have developed into a powerful theory of translation and, more widely, interlingual intercultural mediation. The models (incorporating the linguistic, kinetic/typographic and paralinguistic/graphic components of every speech act), as yet unpublished in their present form, are explained in Viaggio (1998) and my forthcoming pieces.
4. This, I submit, should put pseudo translations squarely in their place — i.e. outside translation theory, if as a potentially interesting epiphenomenon.
5. Let me explain what such identity is: You and I both see the pencil you have in front of you from different angles and distances; maybe you are daltonic and cannot make out its colour; but both you and I see the same pencil. In this sense and despite their differences, our perceptions are, nevertheless, relevantly identical. On the other hand, if I ask you for the red pencil — which, you, as colour-blind, cannot tell from the green one next to it — our perceptions are no longer relevantly identical and communication cannot prosper. In order for it to succeed, we must find perceptual identity through some other means (viz, that I ask you for the long pencil, or the one on your right, etc.). This is what normally happens in everyday communication: little by little we correct our aiming until we finally hit that target which is relevant identity between the perception I want to convey and the one you get. Barring mostly trivial cases, this identity, unfortunately, is impossible to prove empirically, both in direct and mediated communication.

References

Chesterman, A. (1997) *Memes of Translation*. Amsterdam and Philadelphia: Benjamins.
García Landa, M. (1990) A general theory of translation (and of language). *Meta* 35, 476–88.
García Landa, M. and Viaggio, S. (forthcoming) *Teoría general de la traducción*.
Simeoni, D. (1998) The pivotal status of the translator's habitus. *Target* 10, 1–39.
Viaggio, S. (1998) Textual equivalence of perceptual identity? García Landa's model, the
    status of equivalence, and the hermeneutics and heuristics of interlingual intercultural
    mediation. In W. Teubert, E. Tognini Bonelli and N. Volz (eds) *Proceedings of the Third
    European Seminar 'Translation and Equivalence'* (pp. 205–11). Mannheim: Institut für
    deutsche Sprache.
Viaggio, S. (forthcoming) Facing the third millennium. Towards a comprehensive view
    of translation.
Viaggio, S. (forthcoming) The teacher as setter of professional norms. Some thoughts on
    quality in simultaneous interpretation. *Rivista Internazionale di Tecnica della Traduzione.*
Viaggio, S. (forthcoming) The García Landa/Viaggio general theory and models of
    translation and interlingual intercultural mediation. *TEXTconTEXT.*

Some of Us Are Finally Talking to Each Other. Would it Mark the Beginning of a True Dialogue? Comments on Responses

Gideon Toury

As the Aston Seminar was drawing to its end, I felt that we had not really talked about the specific topic of 'Translation and Norms'. We spoke about quite a lot of different topics, as evidenced in the transcribed and edited debates, but these were not always directly relevant to the actual point of the Seminar. I also felt that we did not have a discussion in the proper sense of the word.

The organisers' idea to contact a number of colleagues who had not been to Aston and ask them to respond to the two position papers certainly bore worthwhile fruit. In his own way, each respondent indeed made me rethink something, be it a theoretical issue, a methodological point, or even an element of the rhetoric of presentation, which, as I have come to realise, deserves a lot more attention than I used to give it, especially as the dividing line between a rhetorical device and the contents it may be carrying is not all that sharp. At any rate, it is a fact that the former is often read as if it not only carried, but actually *was* the latter. As I have always been notoriously slow in processing novelties, the results of my rethinking will find their expression in future work. I have no doubt about that. I trust this delay will be amply compensated by thoroughness.

One strategic conclusion already drawn is that I will have to remind myself more often, not only that the language I am writing in is not really mine (which I have always been sorely aware of), but that I am addressing audiences whose majority likewise has English as a foreign language. It is not necessarily the same brand of English either, nor does it always represent the same kind of foreignness. Here is one revealing example:

Until I saw Douglas Robinson analyse my use of the phrase 'scholars wishing to get to the bottom' (note 3), it hadn't occurred to me that anyone would regard this rhetorical device as a theoretical point in disguise. Much less so had it occurred to me that the activity referred to by that cliché would be visualised as 'digging' (why not 'diving', for example?), let alone removing 'rubble' piling on top of something, or that the (desired or factual?) termination of that activity would be interpreted as hitting 'pay-dirt'.

What I did, in fact, was much simpler. It was also closely related to how I chose the word 'paragraphs' to cover my mode of presentation (see 'Introductory Note' to my position paper), and hence part of a unified rhetorical strategy: I proceeded from a Hebrew expression and started looking for an English habitual replacement, one that would be a normal choice among Hebrew-English bilinguals.

The expression I was toying with, *la-redet le-xeqer*, seemed particularly appropriate, in the present context, among other things — because it has the word *xeqer* in it, which, in most modern uses, would mean 'research'. The idiomatic meaning of this cliché is something like 'reach thorough understanding', but literally it reads 'go down until (full) understanding (has been reached)'. Thus, it certainly embodies the same directionality as the English replacement I chose, maybe a similar finality as well (to the extent that knowledge would be regarded as gold, which the Hebrew idiom does not necessarily imply). At any rate, that's about all the two idioms share, as far as their verbal formulation goes.

I would have thought Robinson, for one, would appreciate this playful method of coming up with linguistic formulations, knowing for sure (because we have had an opportunity to compare notes) that, if there is one thing the two of us share, it is the desire to have fun while doing scholarly work and reporting about it. *Jeu de mots* certainly has a prominent position among those things that I get my kicks out of, bilingual punning included. I thought Robinson would appreciate, maybe even share this predilection of mine, which could also be taken as an open test of tolerance for multiculturalism, so highly valued nowadays; at least in theory. I was obviously very wrong.

Bilingual punning as a technique of verbal formulation is of course known to have been applied by many speakers, writers and, yes, translators; whether it is done deliberately or inadvertently (and the borderline between the two tends to erode anyway: a habit easily becomes a second nature). Under certain, basically sociocultural circumstances — for example, in a group whose members all have the same languages — recourse to this technique may even gain preference, nor would such preference necessarily stop where the individual ends.

Thus, on occasion, bilingual punning becomes so regular within a group of this kind that it may be said to represent what to me is 'norm-governed behaviour'; almost to the extent of 'the more, the better'. What is no less important, under such circumstances: this is the way an utterance would also be approached and interpreted within the 'contract' tying together speakers/writers and listeners/readers, namely on the basis of the dual assumption that, while it certainly is an intended utterance in language A, it also represents a (possible or existing) utterance in language B. In fact, much like the way I suggested translated texts be approached, if one's wish is to proceed from the (relatively observable) results of acts of behaviour and reconstruct the (less observable) acts which yielded them and the (even less observable) constraints under which the decisions were made (Toury, 1995: Chapter 3). If this assumption is not activated in full, at least as a *hypothesis*, textually possible but (for the non-post-modernist I am) contextually unjustified interpretations may ensue, often of much greater consequence than Robinson's finding pay-dirt in my bottom (pun intended).

Yes, in a (retrospective, post-factum) scholarly context norms are to be regarded as hypotheses, tentatively tying together ([results of] acts of) behaviour and the circumstances under which they were performed or came into being. As such, their existence is a function of their *explanatory power*, once a certain set of assumptions has been accepted and on its basis, which is a matter of degree rather than an either/or issue; a matter of feasibility rather than factuality.

At the same time, I fail to see why norms should not equally be regarded as *entities*; certainly when the direction of observation is reversed (e.g. in prospective thinking about them and their activity such as culture planning), but possibly even within the retrospective framework itself. In my view, being hypothetical and being a phenomenon are not two mutually exclusive statuses. Even if one wishes to regard something as a 'fiction' (which I did not do myself, as far as concerns norms!), it doesn't follow that something is a non-entity. What it would be at most is an entity of a particular standing, although even of that particularity I am not all that sure; and not only as far as 'translation and norms' goes.

For instance, the dividing line between cats and dogs, and hence the distinctness of the categories of 'cat' and 'dog' themselves, even the attribution of individual 'entities' to one of the two categories, would they be 'facts' or 'fictions'? Is my Mitsi 'really' a cat, or is it just a hypothesis of mine? And does not such a hypothesis, even if shared by many, derive from an organised set of assumptions we first had to accept, e.g. a theory? And even if we pretend we have drawn our conclusion on the basis of some observable traits (i.e. lower-level 'facts'), is it not the case that we have been led to look for those traits and ignore others by that same theory? And would we still have the same dividing line (or: would my Mitsi still be [assumed to be] a cat), should we adopt a different zoology (which is the name our theory normally goes under) or drop it altogether? In brief, are we talking realities or hypotheses, entities or fictions? And is the difference all that big?

As I was reading the responses, I had for the first time in a long while (except for isolated cases which still await response and continuation such as Komissarov, 1996; Halverson, 1997; Simeoni, 1998) the impression that some of us in Translation Studies have finally started talking to each other. A promising first step towards a much desired dialogue to be sure, but not yet a real dialogue.

We do not share basic assumptions and goals. Sure, but it will never be the case that we will all be interested in doing exactly the same things. This may bother some, but I refuse to be among them. Being less and less of a missionary, I am quite happy with a division of labour; as long as I am not urged to convert either. What seems to me more important for a true dialogue is the ability — and willingness — to take a step backwards and find out what everybody's assumptions and goals really are and how exactly different goals breed different theoretical and methodological stances. After all, as I said in a previous 'Invitation to a New Discussion' (Toury, 1995a: 135):

> Far from being a neutral procedure, establishing an object of study is perforce a function of the theory in whose terms it is constituted, which is always geared to cater for a particular set of needs. Its establishment and justification are therefore intimately connected with the questions one wishes to pose, the possible methods of dealing with the objects of study with an eye to those questions — and, indeed, the kind of answers which would count as admissible. The question is not really what the object *is*, then, but rather what would be taken *to constitute* a proper object, in pursuit of a certain goal, such that any change of approach would entail a change of object. This is so even if all objects superficially fall under the same heading; be it even 'translation' and 'translating' themselves. It is not the *label* that counts, but the concept it applies to; and *concepts* can only be established within conceptual *networks*.

Obviously, this holds true only in as much as what we are interested in is indeed research, empirical or theoretical, and hence are obliged to perform the concomitant activity of establishing an object for study; in theory as well as in practice. Some may not be interested in that at all, and dialogue with those will necessarily be much harder.

Be that as it may, as the quote goes on,

> the fallacious rejection of somebody else's concepts on the grounds that they are untenable within one's own frame of reference, which was designed to serve a completely different purpose, is still very much with us. (ibid)

Basically, this is still the case. Luckily, there seem to be first signs of change now. Where we will find ourselves in their wake, only time will tell.

References

Halverson, S. (1997) The concept of equivalence in translation studies: Much ado about something. *Target* 9, 207–33.

Komissarov, V.N. (1996) Assumed translation: Continuing the discussion. *Target* 8, 365–74.

Simeoni, D. (1998) The pivotal status of the translator's habitus. *Target* 10, 1–39.

Toury, G. (1995) *Descriptive Translation Studies and Beyond*. Amsterdam and Philadelphia: Benjamins.

Toury, G. (1995a) The notion of 'assumed translation': An invitation to a new discussion. In H. Bloemen, E. Hertog and W. Segers (eds) *Letterlijkheid Woordelijkheid: Literality Verbality* (pp. 135–47). Antwerpen and Hermelen: Fantom.

Some Concluding Comments on the Debates and the Responses

Theo Hermans

It is surprising that the notion of equivalence should have loomed so large in the debate. In my paper the discussion of equivalence constitutes little more than a rearguard action. The suggestion was that the logic of working with a norms concept must inevitably lead to scepticism concerning the viability of equivalence. If translation is norm-governed as well as intentional, one-directional and historical, equivalence becomes hard to maintain. Moreover, norms serve to secure values. If translation must filter through the receptor culture's value systems, equivalence becomes impossible to maintain. What needs explaining then is not the nature of translation equivalence, however diluted, but why it is that, despite the overwhelming case against it, equivalence figures prominently in various concepts of translation. My guess is that, in search of answers to that question, we need to trace the history of the conceptualisation of translation in conjunction with writing as intellectual property, the decline of imitative modes and the professionalisation of translating. The fiction of translation equivalence can only arise and survive if it is in the interests of translators and non-translators alike to present a translation as equivalent with its source, and if there is something to be gained from doing so on the grounds of translation being seen as a mere transparent copy, professionally sanitised and reliable because de-socialised and secondary. Whatever the outcome of such an exploration into the social and ideological construction of translation, using the same problematical and loaded term at both the meta-level and the object-level will only blur issues and ensnare the researcher even further.

Perhaps it is not so surprising that the notion of equivalence should have loomed large in the debate. The issue highlights the presence of more than one disciplinary matrix in the field: translating as a profession, and translation as cultural history. When people experience communication problems because they speak in and from different paradigms, translation is required, as Thomas Kuhn pointed out in the 1969 postscript to his *Structure of Scientific Revolutions*; but translation, as we know, is far from simple. Some of the differences in the debate can be reduced to different frames of reference, and to different aims and goals associated with the study of translation. While one side assumes that the commonplaces of modern literary theory are common knowledge, the other side cannot believe that not everyone is conversant with Grice's implicatures. While for some the application of translation theory and history to teaching, criticism and evaluation remains paramount, others, like Gideon Toury, are in pursuit of generalisable laws of translation, while still others, like myself, continue to be intrigued by the theoretical paradoxes and historical complexities of translation.

The issue of norms in the study of translation can probably be taken further in at least two directions. One is methodological. If the heuristic value of the norm concept is to be fully exploited in translation research, we may need to think through such issues as the range of options readily available to translators, the nature of shared expectations, and the selectivity and intentionality of actual translation practice. It seems to me that the question of selectivity has not had the attention it deserves. It cannot be enough to say that a particular option was chosen by a translator or met with approval from an audience because this or that was the norm and the option chosen conformed to it. If we want to assess the significance of translation in its historical, cultural and sociopolitical context, we need to figure out not just what the possible alternatives were (in principle, just about anything is possible) but what the most likely, the most obvious alternatives were, the alternatives that were emphatically not chosen. The significance of a choice lies in its contingency. The illocutionary force of an utterance, its point, can only be gauged against the background of what, in the circumstances, could have been expected but was excluded. Stressing the selectivity of choices can make us see the powerful exclusionary mechanisms at work in the selection of texts for translation, the phrasing of translations, and their deployment at a later stage. Norms themselves suggest preferred options and exclude others. The actual choices which translators — and others — make, signal both inclusions and exclusions in relation to the set of preferred options. We cannot begin to grasp the agenda behind what is given unless we know what was pushed out of sight.

Another direction leads towards the values which norms keep in place. This line takes us into cultural studies and new historicism, and into a critique of the modern ideology of translation. In the past two decades or so we have concentrated on the operational aspect of the norms concept. Norms have been classified into different kinds and used as instruments of analysis or as a link between the individual and the social. The fact that norms secure values and beliefs has received much less attention. Yet this is ultimately what makes translation relevant and interesting.

It is also why manipulation, for all its dark and deliberate overtones, remains a useful term, at the opposite end of transparency, immanent truths and the mechanistic conception of translation. The spin which translation puts on texts even as it claims to speak for them without raising its own voice, can be overt or insidious. Either way it carries the trace of how and where the translating pole positions itself in relation to the source. At a time when the emphasis in translation studies has shifted from prescription and description to the sociocultural, ideological and political effects of translation, the connection between translational norms and values seems a relevant focus.

Each one of us studies translation in a particular institutional environment, with a history behind us, goals to reach and stakes to defend. We translate translation in a disciplined manner, in accordance with the norms and values of the discipline. It is remarkable that the study of translation, concerned as it is with the traffic between different value systems as well as different signifying systems, has shown so little awareness of its own entanglement in these systems. Other disciplines, notably ethnography, have grappled with the weight of their own history, their own language, their own conditions of knowledge and terms of description. Translation studies has taken surprisingly little note of their own epistemological presuppositions and entanglements. Of course, this type of investigation leads to forms of self-reflexive soul-searching that are unlikely to produce results at once satisfactory and practical. But unless we want to claim a bland neutrality and objectivity, or wash our hands of power and complicity, we would do well to be rather more alert than we have been to the presuppositions and entanglements that studying translation involves us in.

The responses by Daniel Gile and Sergio Viaggio, diametrically opposed one to the other, do not leave me much scope for further comments. Daniel Gile favours empirical research, with explicitly formulated hypotheses and strict testing methods. His work has been concerned mostly with cognitive constraints in professional interpreting, and his willingness to try out the usefulness of norms concepts in the study of interpreting is heartening. As for Viaggio, I can only say that I envy but cannot share any of his certainties regarding the essence of translation or the purpose of studying and theorising it. I wonder just how general his and García Landa's general theory of translation is going to be, given Viaggio's blunt dismissal of translation history and literary translation in favour of the corporate interests of today's professional translators and interpreters.

For Douglas Robinson, clearly, I use the word 'clearly' too often, handing him an opportunity for parody. Fine. The computer tells me 'clearly' occurs five times (and 'clear' twice, plus once in a quotation), in an 11,000 words essay. Hardly excessive. I don't mind Robinson enjoying himself at my expense, but it suggests his reading of my text is more than a little self-indulgent.

First a couple of minor points in Robinson's response. My main source for the 'translator function' idea is not Díaz-Diocaretz or Arrojo, let alone Robinson, but Karin Littau, as acknowledged in the essay and in earlier publications (Hermans, 1996a, 1996b). As for the use of 'opaque' in addition to images suggesting deflection and refraction: I want to emphasise with it that translations have a substance of their own, a thickness if you like, which you cannot simply peel away. You may be able to calculate angles of deflection and thus find ways of neutralising its effect. By speaking of opacity I want to suggest that this is not possible with translations because such things as the different values, echoes and histories attaching to the words used, and the hybridity of the discursive subjects in translations, are baked into the texts themselves. And yes, this is what I think makes translation interesting, relevant and revealing, as cultural history. But instead of talking about 'conceptual conflict' here I would call it a paradox, the same paradox that inheres in the attempt to be as clear as possible about opacity. My essay contains other paradoxes; more about those below.

I must take up the alleged methodological slipping and sliding in connection with de Buck. The case is not about the importance of norms or getting inside de Buck's head, but about ways of making sense of de Buck's actions. This implies that I regard his translating and publishing Boethius as a deliberate intervention into a given state of affairs, and I attribute intentionality to his actions, including his speech acts of translating (at a certain time, in a certain way, in two different ways as it turns out — why and with what purpose?) and making statements about his translation (why does he choose to mention the Dutch Republic, why the need to explain that he has translated some parts of his source text differently and what can we make of the exact words he uses and the reasons he gives to describe and justify this different — deviant? — mode of translating?). This is not hermeneutics. If anything it aspires to a form of historiography, the construction of a plausible plot to account for the available evidence, or at least the evidence I regard as (and therefore make) pertinent. Whether this plot reflects a historical reality 'as it was', we shall never know, since all our historical knowledge consists of such plots. And all these plots, especially those devised to answer why-questions, remain conjectures, speculation. Most are based on textual evidence, some of it flimsy and supported by other conjectural knowledge. The fact, incidentally, that so little is known about de Buck as an historical case suits me very well. Since de Buck only serves as an illustration we don't want to be weighed down with a mass of detail. Besides, it is pleasing to see that even an apparently straightforward case like de Buck's still provides the plot-constructing researcher with plenty of leads.

The main tool to probe into the matter is the norms concept, sharpened on two sides, firstly by emphasising the element of expectations as a means of bridging the individual and the social spheres, and secondly by highlighting selectivity and hence also exclusion. The broad idea is that if I have a sense of the array of courses of action that others expect a person to take in certain circumstances, I may be able to grasp the significance of the particular option this person selects from that array. Conversely, if someone feels called upon to provide an explanation justifying why they did x rather than a or b, the implication is they had taken a path that was not the one expected as a matter of course by the relevant group. The idea derives from Luhmann's model of communication, not from Structuralism as Pym seems to think.

In de Buck's case I have taken the translator at his word when he said he wanted to offer consolation. I can't think of a reason not to believe him on that score. If we accept de Buck's claim that he wanted to provide consolation (as an intervention, a response to a situation, an answer to a problem which he perceived, as indeed he tells us, and which I perceive him perceiving), I think it is reasonable to assume different courses of action were open to him. So I speculate about what may account for the decision to translate, and I use the notion of expectations in reviewing obvious alternatives. Next, picking a relevant text to translate. What texts came into consideration? We can't know for certain but, yes, I am pretty sure Lipsius' *De constantia* was among them, given that book's thematic suitability, status and availability. The choice for Boethius (and hence against Lipsius and an indeterminate number of other alternatives) brings with it several subsequent decisions, some no doubt more convention- or norm-governed than others. De Buck may, for instance, have had a free choice in deciding whether to offer a full or a truncated version, but placing Boethius outside a Catholic framework cannot have been a realistic option in view of prevailing censorship laws. Then the mode of translating. Why two modes within one book, why de Buck's comments on one of them, and what can we infer from the terms he uses to describe it? True, in my account I don't put all the evidence about 'prevailing modes' on the table. Readers are asked to take that on trust, as they are asked to accept that the historical circumstances of de Buck's translation were roughly as I sketched them, and that I did not simply invent de Buck (a distinct possibility). But Robinson can be assured I have evidence to support what I say about paraphrase in the seventeenth century — *not* in any transhistorical sense — in Western Europe generally and in the Low Countries in particular (in case he's worried: Hermans, 1985, 1987, 1991, 1992, 1996c, 1997a). The reasons I advance in connection with the presence of two variant translations side by side are entirely conjectural, and I warn the reader about this. I relate them to norms, conventions and expectations, and interpret de Buck's choices as signalling (whether intentional or not on de Buck's part) a number of other things which involve other cultural and political tensions. Not everyone may be convinced by my conjectures. If someone devises a more plausible explanation, I'll put mine in the bin. But methodologically I maintain the procedure is sound.

When I wrote my 'Translation and Normativity' essay I had not read Anthony Pym's *Method in Translation History*, although I had seen some chapters in manuscript about eighteen months earlier. Had I read it (as I have now), it would not have made any difference. Pym criticises some aspects of the norms concept as it has been used in descriptive research, but his points are not relevant to my paper. I am puzzled by Robinson's statement that 'as Pym makes clear, part of the problem underlying norms research as it is practised by DTSers like Toury and Hermans is that it aspires to the status of an empirical or objective or positive science, when norms (unlike, say, rocks) have no positive existence to be empirically described'. I don't think Pym's book says what Robinson makes it say, but let's leave that aside. Norms, as psycho-social entities, are not directly observable. Gravity, grammar and guilt have no 'positive existence' (whatever that is) either, yet few people doubt their relevance. It is conceivable that Gideon Toury views translation studies as aspiring to 'an empirical or objective or positive science' (he will speak for himself; I criticised his positivist streak in Hermans, 1995), but the descriptive approach accommodates more diversity than Robinson's facile gloss suggests. If Robinson had done more than jump on the word 'clear' and decide in passing we should all take lessons from a gallery of greats comprising Nietzsche, Freud, Burke and Robinson, he might have realised that the argument in my essay points in the opposite direction from positivism, towards the recognition of epistemological paradoxes, complexities, aporias and ironies besetting the study of translation. The notion of 'translating translation' is one aspect of this. The unease I feel with regard to contemporary researchers' unquestioning use of 'equivalence' is another, as is my interest in constructivist epistemologies like Luhmann's. I am aware that these paradoxes rebound on my own statements about translation, and that therefore my account of de Buck cannot be a transparent translation. In an earlier text, where the issue was raised only briefly, I alerted the audience to this irony (Hermans, 1997b). In the essay in the present volume I thought this would be redundant because the inference seemed, well, crystal-clear.

Andrew Chesterman and Anthony Pym have made more of an effort to engage with Gideon's and my work, even though some of Pym's sniping is of the Robinson variety. Pym has detected changes in the way Gideon Toury and I write about translation. I am not greatly concerned whether the things I have been saying about translation in recent years are post- or pre- or metamodern, but the change has been rather less abrupt than Pym thinks. I recall writing that 'all translation implies a degree of manipulation of the source text for a certain purpose' in 1985 (*Manipulation of Literature*, Introduction). Never mind. It is what Pym says about my postmodern fall from grace that is remarkable. He suspects it is a matter of 'theories read rather than translations studied'. In the overwhelmingly conservative translations he deals with he can find no 'refractory increase in voices, perspectives and meanings' and all that. My comments about this 'refractory increase', he writes, are 'certainly not a series of hypotheses awaiting falsification' but 'a sleight of hand' attributing active verbs to translations as things. As for the active verbs: what drivel — surely Pym has heard of the word 'metaphor'? In any case, the de Buck example, to look no further, offers a glaring illustration of a refractory increase in voices, perspectives and meanings as it superimposes de Buck's local, temporalised, polemical, conservative, intertextual voice on that of Boethius. Its echoes comprise decades of Counter-Reformation polemic, a thousand years of philological commentary on Boethius, the rhetorical genre of consolation, the literature and learning of the Dutch Republic, and more. No refractory increase? In an earlier article, very much concerned with 'translations studied' (Hermans, 1996a), I argued in some detail for recognising a translator's voice in translations. Of course these analyses are based on theories read — what else would they be based on? On translations studied just like that, without a theoretical angle? If that is what Pym means by method in translation history we might begin to understand why his recent book of that title ('horizon-expanding', Robinson tells us) can't be bothered even to mention theoretical debates among historians about writing history. Shall I assume that his own concepts of regimes and interculturality are not theoretical concepts either? Perhaps they are hypotheses awaiting falsification? No, regime theory, or norm theory, or systems theory, or deconstruction for that matter, are ways of focusing attention, of asking questions, of locating data. New theories, new questions, new data. They are lines of approach, vantage points, searchlights. None of them claims to be comprehensive, or the last word.

Pym's questions as to how norms change and what variables enter into the process are more serious, and too large. Two considerations seem quite obvious to me. One, approaching translation history or translators' behaviour via norms can only be a way into the matter, no more than a starting point. It will not in itself deliver a comprehensive or even a very interesting picture. The attempt to do a bit of 'reverse engineering' on translators' decisions is bound to lead to other and broader categories — political, economic, ideological, ethical, cultural, religious, whatever. In my de Buck example I highlighted some of these categories as determining factors, as 'values' underpinning sets of norms. How many, and which ones, are relevant? How many variables to include, where and when? The answer bears on the other consideration that seems obvious to me: it will depend on the angle from which, or the lens through which, one looks at the case. Even the perception of change, I suggest, depends on this. What looks like disruption from one point of view may appear as continuity from another. Searchlights illuminate certain things and not others, and they are operated from certain positions. Values inform not only the way we translate but also the way we look at translation. I like to think that this is the idea that holds the two parts of my essay in this volume together. Translation and the study of translation are both cultural practices.

Andrew Chesterman has made use of norms concepts in his own work. It surprises me therefore that he should think that having the term 'norm' refer to both regularities in behaviour and the underlying mechanism constitutes a 'category mistake'. There is no mistake: the double use of the term may be confusing in some respects, but (a) it conforms to common usage and (b) it follows directly from my starting point, which is to anchor norms in the notion of convention as formally defined by David Lewis ('A regularity R in the behavior of members of a population P ... is a convention if and only if ...').

Chesterman is right to suggest that there is no need to think about equivalence in binary terms, as either there or not there. The proposal he made regarding similarity (Chesterman, 1996) is of interest, but in his response here he spoils his case by invoking Newmark's comments about translation as approximation. Newmark's reference is to the idea of translation as the closest natural equivalent, as striving towards identity but being content with approximation. The implication there is that ideally translation ought to be able to coincide with its source, alas in practice it always falls short. Difference then is imperfection and want, something to be overcome, an original sin in search of a baptismal font. This strikes me as not just a utopian and metaphysical concept of translation, but one which obliges us to speak of translation as negativity, as constantly in need of replenishment. Hence my emphasis on difference as given, and as revealing in its own right. Yes, in many pragmatic situations translation does manage to effectuate a form of communication by being 'relevantly similar', but it is effective only because the participants selectively suppress dissimilarity. There is nothing wrong with that, indeed communication would not be possible without it. But it is not the whole story, and so in a discourse about translation which claims scholarly and critical status we should think twice about adopting blanket terms like 'equivalence'. My comments about equivalence and about 'translating translation' are invitations to reflect about the assumptions and the vocabulary of translation studies, attempts at consciousness-raising, if you like.

This brings me to the final section of Chesterman's comments, on 'Theory'. Earlier in his response, in the section on 'Value', Chesterman points out that my statement about translations never being value-free is surely a platitude. I agree. But it is a platitude which many conceptions, or ideologies, of translation routinely deny. The view of translation as approximation-forever-striving-to-wards-identity has no room for it. In addition, several linguistic and also descriptive approaches to translation commonly sidestep the issue, whether by focusing exclusively on formal linguistic categories or by claiming that description must exclude evaluation. My statements about theory try to face up to the complexity and irony of our speaking about translation. I have no problem with theorising for its own sake, as an end in itself. I don't share Gideon's view that theory is relevant only insofar as it feeds into specific case studies. Rather, I see a critical role for theoretical reflection as folding back on theories of translation — including contemporary theories, including the presuppositions of translation studies. This may well be light-years away from the real-life problems of professional translators, as Chesterman puts it. Perhaps. I agree with Gideon that it is not the primary task of translation studies to interfere directly (note 'primary' and 'directly', Chesterman forgets this) with how translators go about their business. But I would argue, against Gideon, that the matter is not that simple. However descriptively or theoretically cocooned some forms of translation study may want to be, they interact with other branches of the field and, indirectly, at several removes perhaps, but still, with practice — e.g. to the extent that sooner or later translator training courses take account of some aspects of descriptive or theoretical or other work, or to the extent that changing practices of translation, e.g. in a multi-media environment, generate different discourses which must eventually impact on even the most ethereal theorising. Light-years maybe, but light travels.

Another aspect of this self-reflexive theorising is that it denies any strict separation between historical thinking about translation and contemporary thinking, whether it claims scholarly status or not. This points, among other things, to the contingency of notions and terminologies of translation current in translation studies. There lies the aporia, and the irony, of translation studies as I see it, and hence of my own speaking in this context. How such metatheoretical reflection might translate into practice, Chesterman asks. Should translators translate differently? No. Translators do as they do. But people engaged in studying translation might do well to look at the way in which historians, or sociologists, or, as I suggested, anthropologists, have struggled with the entanglement of their disciplines with their respective objects. It would not be such a bad idea to see how, say, Clifford Geertz' thick description, or the more postmodern forms of ethnography, or Hayden White's narrativity, or Stephen Greenblatt's new historicism, or Bourdieu's fields, or indeed Luhmann's anti-foundationalist epistemology, might be applied to translation issues. It would bring new life and fresh challenges into the discipline. The poverty of current translation studies, it seems to me, is their failure to elaborate a theoretical apparatus that comes anywhere near to doing justice to the historical relevance and conceptual complexity of translation. That is why I think the discipline needs impulses from other areas of study as well as critical inspection of its own operations and vocabulary.

References

Chesterman, A. (1996) On similarity. *Target* 8, 159–64.
Hermans, T. (1985) Vondel on translation. *Dutch Crossing* 26, 38–72.
Hermans, T. (1987) Huygens on translation. *Dutch Crossing* 33, 3–27.
Hermans, T. (1991) Translating 'Rhetorijckelijck' or 'Ghetrouwelijck'. Some contexts of Dutch renaissance approaches to translation. In T. Hermans and R. Salverda (eds) *Standing Clear. Festschrift R.P. Meijer* (pp. 151–72). London: Centre for Low Countries Studies.
Hermans, T. (1992) Renaissance translation between literalism and imitation. In H. Kittel (ed.) *Geschichte, System, Literarische Übersetzung/Histories, Systems, Literary Translations* (pp. 95–116). Berlin: Erich Schmidt.
Hermans, T. (1995) Toury's empiricism version one. *The Translator* 1, 215–23.
Hermans, T. (1996a) The translator's voice in translated narrative. *Target* 8, 23–48.
Hermans, T. (1996b) Translation's other. Inaugural Lecture, University College London.
Hermans, T. (ed.) (1996c) *Door eenen engen hals. Nederlandse beschouwingen over vertalen 1550–1670*. The Hague: Bibliographia Neerlandica.
Hermans, T. (1997a) The task of the translator in the European renaissance. Explorations in a discursive field. In S. Bassnett (ed.) *Translating Literature* (pp. 14–40). Cambridge: D.S. Brewer.
Hermans, T. (1997b) Translation as institution. In M. Snell-Hornby *et al.* (eds) *Translation as Intercultural Communication* (pp. 3–20). Amsterdam and Philadelphia: Benjamins.